The Frolicking Physio

To Catherine and Ron

Many thanks for
all your help.

Best Wishes
Blair :)

BLAIR FARISH

 www.trafford.com

North America & international
toll-free: 1 888 232 4444 (USA & Canada)
phone: 250 383 6864 ♦ fax: 812 355 4082

Book Cover Design by Craig Farish and Ryan Lawrence

Photos included clockwise from top right: Blair on Nipissing Lake, North Bay, Ontario, at -30 degrees centigrade; Blair on first Scooter, age 5: Sgt. Farish, Kinrara, Malaya, 1961: Maimie and Nana, Broombush, 1958: Walkabout in Australia, Blair, 1985: Wedding Day Maureen and Blair, August 7th, 1997 on Vespa.

Pencil sketches by the author.

Dedication

With love and gratitude to Maureen and our precious family. Written as a keepsake for our ten grandchildren.

Acknowledgement

A special thanks is due to Catherine Nelson for much appreciated editing assistance provided at the cost of a couple of bottles of her favourite red wine. Also thanks to Jocelyn Fast for her many hours of typing.

Table of Contents

My Chosen Career

*T*he first salvo of the barrage that was to come struck quickly. I crouched involuntarily as the question was barked, "Name?"

Momentarily, in a fog of fear, I hesitated then plucked up my courage and answered, "Oh, 'er, Blair."

"First Name?" the voice barked again.

I cringed and apologetically offered, "Oh that is my Christian name. My family name is Farish."

This provoked a sharp response. "Well why didn't you say that in the first place?"

The enemy in that baptism of fire was Sergeant McGregor*. As communications expert and senior executive, he was the sole occupant of the Dumfries recruiting station for the King's Own Scottish Borderers (K.O.S.B.), the local regiment.

Above the left breast pocket of his battledress tunic were two rows of medals which I later learned were evidence of his attendance and active participation in several theatres of war. He'd been around in his twenty years. He'd seen service with the Desert Rats in North Africa, at the relief of Nimagen, in Palestine, at the Mau Mau uprising in Kenya, on a barren hill in Korea and at a parachute drop in Suez. Added to this were medals of valour and long service and good conduct. He obviously deserved, but I'm sure had not requested, the peacefulness and boredom of being put out to pasture with the title of 'Recruiting Officer' in his home town in southern Scotland.

It was late June in 1957 and the memories of past times of glory did little to improve his demeanour as he peered at the spotty-faced eighteen year old potential recruit. My presence in that stuffy, smoke-filled little office was my final choice following a year of exasperation.

The previous year on, July 8th, I had stumbled out of my sixth year at Dumfries Academy, totally shocked that despite the gloom and doom predictions of my teachers, I had achieved the unexpected exam results granting me a university entrance qualification. That caught me ill prepared for embarking on any meaningful career choice of further education, as I had set my sights on completing the compulsory two year conscription into military service that faced every eighteen year old male at that time.

Regrettably, the powers that be had bogged down the process of call-up and I'd spent a whole year doing fill-in jobs in what might now be described as a 'gap' year. As the first anniversary of leaving school approached, I'd had enough of waiting. It was with a sense of exasperation that I'd plucked up the courage to come face-to-face with the much-medaled man.

Spying what he perceived as an easy catch, the sergeant settled down to spit out a few cursory questions about my general health, education and work experience. Six month stints as a farm labourer and temporary postman didn't impress him much. "You haven't exactly strained yourself in the past year, have you?" I shrugged in response, but his assurance that I could be in the army within a week made me overlook his belittling comment.

He reached back to the shelf that contained three or four impressive manuals which were the only signs of industry thereabouts. "You're a local lad, so it'll be the K.O.S.B. for you." I suspected that he'd get bonus points for his entrapment of another volunteer for his own regiment. He scowled as I quickly shot down enrolment into the infantry. He tried again. "Okay then, you're a big boy, you'll do fine in the Scot's Guards."

With his mention of that elite brigade I could see myself standing in front of Buckingham Palace, in my kilt and furry bearskin hat (it was before the onslaught of animal right's complaints). People would be poking and gaggling about what was worn beneath the kilt. "Oh, no Mr. McGregor, I couldn't, I wouldn't want that."

"You'll address me as Sergeant, laddie," he said. Not bothering to enquire about what I had in mind, he went on. "Ok, Parachute Regiment, Marines..." I cut him off with the idea that I'd like to go into the Medical Corps. I didn't want to divulge that my recent meeting with, and fondness for, a special wee Scottish lass who was a nurse, had something to do with that decision.

Silence fell heavily between us. Scorn came over his ruddy countenance. I'm sure he'd appreciated the medics' proximity when he was battling at Panmunjom on the 38th Parallel, but his thoughts at that moment were obviously that real men go into a regiment, although he didn't need to say it.

With a shrug of resignation he chose another less thumb-marked manual that related to my choice of enlistment. He perused the pages for a few moments then lifted his eyes to stare me down. "You need a school leaving certificate to get into any of these jobs." He seemed disappointed when I reminded him that I'd definitely gone well past the standard school leaving age of fifteen in those days.

"Nurse? You'll make a fine nurse." The sarcasm was evident in his tone. He took my lack of response to mean no, and moved down the list. "Laboratory technician?" My youthful image of the bottles of urine and heaps of other unmentionable excreta finished that discussion. He didn't even lift his eyes but moved on. "Radiographer?"

There was a momentary intrigue of the unknown as my ignorance of medical matters made me ask, "What's that?"

His finger moved slowly along the line. "That's x-rays, and things like that." My horror showed, as I guessed that x-rays and sterility went hand in hand and further misconstrued that sterility and impotence might be connected. I quickly ruled out that option.

I could tell I was straining his patience. His voice took on a new sharp edge. "Physiotherapy?" He stumbled over the word. I had never heard of that work so I asked for further information. He read a few lines that gave scant, unintelligible descriptions.

"That's exercise, and hydrotherapy and electrotherapy and things like that." I was still lost in this high-falutin' mumbo jumbo, when suddenly his eyes brightened up. He looked positively human for a moment.

"The coach at Queen for the South football team is a physiotherapist."

The Sergeant had my undivided attention. Football, (soccer to North Americans) had been my addiction, the main reason for living, and the one thing I had excelled in, all through school. I had a rush of enthusiasm and cut him off before he could change his mind. "Oh that sounds great," I said.

He stopped me short. "There's only a select few get into that sort of thing."

I was forewarned but now determined. "This is the one I want," I stated firmly.

He looked me over again, doing some sort of private evaluation. Then he picked up the pen and wrote the magic word on the sheet before him.

The rest of the interview and questions meant little to me. I sailed through the next few minutes oblivious. Nothing else mattered because I had decided. The assurance and confidence reserved only for those with the exuberance and naivety of youth, cemented the deal.

Two days later I had a full medical exam. I tolerated a chest-x-ray (with some suspicion), peed in the proffered bottle and was declared as healthy as a horse, except for one thing.

"Oh, oh!" the examining doctor said. "You are a lucky one. You've got flat feet. Every National Serviceman prays for feet like yours. You're exempt."

I almost cried. "But there is nothing wrong with my feet! They never hurt, I play football three times a week, I cycle miles, and I run everywhere. You've got to let me join up. I'm going to be a physiotherapist."

He stood back, astonished at the sight of somebody pleading to join the army when every other eighteen year old was trying every trick in the book to avoid conscription. "I don't know laddie," he said. "We get terrible trouble with flat-footers doing drill and marching all day, but, well, if you are as keen as all that, I'll write you up as painless flat feet."

My family was less than impressed when I told that I had signed on for three years because I didn't want to waste more time waiting for National Service call up, but they supported my choice.

Two days later a smiling Sergeant McGregor personally handed me my enlistment papers and train ticket to Aldershot, home of the British Army. (My actual destination was just outside Aldershot at Crookham, the Royal Army Medical Corps (R.A.M.C.) training depot.) Sergeant McGregor's happy expression was no doubt due to his having filled his quota of one regular volunteer enlistment per week. He even called me, Blair, but I knew better than to ask him for his first name.

Family and friends were there to see me off at Dumfries railway station at 11:20 pm that very Thursday evening. I was blissfully unaware of the sad historical connection earlier generations tied to that late night train. Known as the 'heart breaker', the overnight train to London had taken away thousands of local young men and women during the two world wars and many had never returned. For me, on that night in 1957, I was only aware of anticipation and excitement and the knowledge that my life was about to change.

Half a century later, as I talk with students enquiring about a career in physiotherapy, I remember Sergeant McGregor's warning that, "There's only a select few get into that sort of thing," and credit his assistance, albeit unintentional, in pin-holing me to make the selection of my chosen career. He was one of the many individuals who played an important role in my path through life.

Nana's Gift

A smile is just a little thing,
It doesn't cost a jot,
It's free to beggar and to king,
So why not smile a lot?

Often quoted by Mary Porteus Bell Farish

Nana is the affectionate name used to address beloved grandmothers in Scotland. For me, it was one of my earliest memories of childhood utterances. It was spoken to that source of encyclopedic knowledge, patience, encouragement, love and nurturing, my Nana.

Born in 1880, Mary Porteus Bell, the youngest of four sisters in a family of seven children, grew up on the shores of the Solway Firth, that jutting extension of the Irish Sea that tries to separate Scotland from England. Mary survived the overcrowding and hardships of the time, learning that hard work, frugality, and caring for others were what made the world go around.

I recall her tales of childhood days, the two-mile walk to school in Annan, sharing a bed with three sisters, collecting flotsam from the sea and river to fuel the one fire heating the house. She told of scouring the seashore for hermit crabs and tramping in the frigid shallows bare footed to feel for flounders, the flat bottom-fish. Once trapped beneath the searching feet, a flounder could be speared with a sharp rod and proudly taken home to feed the regularly hungry nine mouths of the family.

At twelve years of age, Mary was forced to leave school to work for her living. She joined her older sisters in the most common work of the time as an apprentice seamstress. She must have been a star pupil, as at age seventeen, she was indentured as a junior seamstress in the prestigious 'Barbour's Gentlemen and Ladies Clothiers and Outfitters' on Buccleugh Street in Dumfries. Her work there was to make the required alterations and fittings to apparel purchased by the gentry and aristocracy who patronized that illustrious fashion wear establishment.

Amongst those using Barbour's as their source of custom wear was a patron of substantial means and appropriate birthright, who regularly requested Mary Bell as her personal seamstress. It was Mary she wanted to finalize the fit of her elegant ball gowns and frippery. Soon, due to Mary's skills, as well as the monetary value of the customer's standing, Mr. Barbour the owner of the establishment, had a perplexing dilemma before him. This involved the trade-off of losing his best seamstress in order to please one of his most influential and affluent patrons.

Mary was embarrassingly present during the conversation. Eye-boggled, silent and still as a statue, she heard the Lady say, "Mr. Barbour, I am at pains to ask that you'd be so kind as to dismiss

Mary Bell from your own service and permit me to engage her as my full-time seamstress at my home at Drumpark."

I guarantee the wording of this statement, as Nana would often quote that short, life-changing sentence over the next half a century. She could put on the Victorian upper class accent to a tee.

"For you, Lady Blair, without a moment's hesitation, yes. I am so honoured that you ask this of me." I'm sure under his breath he added, "And it will cost you dearly, Dearie." Nana could in future years, dig deep to duplicate Mr. Barbour's bass tone and his educated Scot's phraseology.

The arrangement must have worked out well, as Mary Bell's respect and admiration for her new employer would influence the selection of the name for her first grandson, yours truly, forty years later.

Ensconced in the servants' quarters in the baronial country home, Mary was well appreciated. She thrived in the unimaginable wealth and splendor of that great household. It was a new world to her, in the company of the butler, chef, chambermaids, matron, chauffeur, governess, gardeners and the French maid.

On Nana's knee as a child, I couldn't get enough of the stories about life in 'the big hoose'. Later as a teenager, taking French at school, who else but Nana would bring out yet another surprise with her unexpected gems of wisdom? "Bon Jour, comment ca va? Merci beaucoup." The accent was quite Parisian, in her imitation of her fellow employee's rendition fifty years earlier.

Of course, the fairy tale story would not be complete without the full saga of boy meets girl. Even an ancestral home, when it reaches its second century, requires renovations and repairs. Just as the Blair family of Drumpark only frequented Barbour's for clothing, they were equally discerning in their choice of tradesmen. Joseph Farish and Sons, Joiners and Undertakers, Painters and Decorators were the carpenters entrusted with the work to make discrete yet meticulous alterations to the Blair ancestral home. Established as a business in 1818, the company's years of experience and excellent local reputation were influential in their success in contracting the work.

Handsome, thirty year old, fourth generation successor in the family business, skilled, meticulous in detail, and hardworking, John Neilson Farish was in the right place at the right time. As was the custom in those days, his willingness and good work were occasionally rewarded with the offering of lunch in the great house kitchen, no doubt to the chagrin of the chef. And so, providentially, pretty young seamstress met handsome young joiner.

On a visit to Scotland over ninety years after the event, I took Maureen past the still impressive Drumpark to the nearby Routen Brig, overlooking a tumbling cascade. There, trout and salmon leapt the falls, and daffodils and rhododendrons painted the ultimate romantic scene. "This is where Grandpa John got down on one knee to ask Nana to be his wife."

I wonder if Bobby Darren heard about this place and what happened there when he wrote and sang many years after that special occasion:

If I were a carpenter, and you were a lady,
Would you marry me anyway, would you have my baby?

By 1904, Grandpa John had purchased two adjoining, tiny, two-room cottages near the banks of the River Cairn. He converted them into a substantial, granite walled, three-bedroom, two-storey home ready for his new wife. Over the next decade, just as the song predicted, they had four children to fill those bedrooms. The house reconstruction in readiness for his new bride, cost two hundred fifty pounds in 1904, and while the house passed from the family in the early 80's, its recent resale in 2004 was for two hundred fifty thousand pounds.

Accustomed to shared servants' quarters at Drumpark House, Nana must have thought she'd arrived in a palace, but by today's standards, things were still quite primitive. The outhouse toilet located fifty yards behind the house seemed a thousand miles away on a jet black night, especially in the wind and rain. It was still so during my fifteen years living there in the 1940's and 50's.

Water for all the cooking, drinking and washing had to be fetched from a small stream one hundred yards distant. Washing hung on an outside clothes-line for days at a time, awaiting some semblance of drying. The finishing touch required draping on a ceiling line in the kitchen. The disposable diaper was still three-quarters of a century away! Heating was coaxed out of the solitary multi-purpose cooking fireplace located in the kitchen. Cold running tap water, electricity and a telephone were the new fangled magic brought in during the late 30's.

Nana nurtured her family through two world wars, the National Strike of the 20's and the hungry 30's. By the time I arrived she was rejuvenated and ready to lavish on me love, generosity, and all the leisure time that she had been denied in her preceding forty years. I was her gift to spoil and pamper. Her gifts to me, a million sacrifices and treasures. She was my professor, nurse, teacher, philosopher, spiritual guide, instructor and inspirational figure. No task was ever too much for my Nana.

Grandpa had been a belated Victorian autocrat, a stern father. He was an elder of the Kirk and a radical teetotaler. By the standards of the day, he was a good father. Perhaps the news of his unwed daughter being, 'with child' was just too much for him in 1938. Coincidental to my birth in Ayr, seventy miles away, where my mother had been banished to produce the offspring, grandpa had a massive stroke and never did recover. My eventual entry to the family home happened only after his death four years later.

Nana had anguished every moment until my belated homecoming. She had such a pent up store of love that my arrival signaled an unleashing of extravagance and joy in her life. If ever a lad was spoiled, it was I.

My mother was the sole income provider and worked half a dozen part-time jobs to make ends meet. She was not acknowledged as my mother until just prior to my departure for the army. Consequently, she was not really a large part of my day-to-day upbringing, and hid from the stigma of my 'disreputable' birth circumstances while Nana became my legal guardian.

In those years, Nana, my mother who I addressed as Maimie, (her adopted abbreviation of Mary Elizabeth Bell Farish) and I made up the household. My three uncles, Dick, Joe and Bill were away from home for the war years. One was machine-gunning his way through Sicily and mainland Italy, another in some clandestine work in ammunition production, and the third a railway stationmaster in bleak Galloway, in the location and the time when John Buchan was penning, *The 39 Steps*. Nana was the fearsome guardian of the home. Who needed men folk?

In her 60's, Nana taught me to fish, snare rabbits, plant a vegetable garden, throttle an old hen, saw logs and chop kindling for the fire. She helped me to learn to read, sing, knit, sew on a button, ride a bike, cook porridge, brew tea and climb a tree. Her guidance got me to dress properly, be polite and mannerly and beyond all that, she gave me the gift of laughter.

In those days, in rural communities despite food rationing and poverty, all visitors were welcome at the door and usually offered a cup of tea and a friendly chat. From time to time a solitary, woebegone figure of a tramp would appear at the door. These were indigent derelicts who would beg for food, the predecessors of today's street people. By habit, I invited one poor waif into the warmth of the kitchen.

A new, almost unrecognizable Nana appeared. She was like a bulldog, fierce and unrelenting and almost physically threw the poor fellow out. Having successfully ejected that bedraggled soul, she ordered him to wait outside. Five minutes later, she returned to give him a huge tomato and lettuce sandwich and filled his metal cup with freshly brewed tea. Afterwards, she took me on her knee and spent ages trying to clarify the confusion I felt over the contradictory banishment and subsequent generosity. The learning went on.

Soon after that incident, I wandered across the road to visit with some young German prisoners-of-war who were doing road cleanup work. They were enthralled with this little blond boy, no doubt thinking of those they'd left behind or lost in their homeland. Again, Nana appeared in full war-paint mode. Her protective instinct at peak, I'm sure she'd have taken on the entire Wermacht single handedly.

Strangely, on that occasion, seeing them harmlessly brewing up a pot of hot chocolate on a small fire, she mellowed and almost sympathized with their plight. She watched as they offered me a small tin of cocoa. Their anxious warning that the cup was hot, "Der kakao ist heiss", brought forth my naïve misinterpretation.

"The cocoa isn't ice, it's hot!" I stated forthrightly. Even Nana joined in their laughter at my innocent 'faux pas'. What a moment to remember forever and hopefully to be recalled by those young soldiers when they returned to their own families in Germany.

As time slipped past, Nana continued to perform her magic, but age was catching up with her. Gradually, I was doing heavier work in the garden, helping transplant lupines and gladioli and those rose bushes that she so loved. I never tired of being her helper and seeing her joy in my being at her side. At seventy, she had developed full-blown rheumatoid arthritis and was just a shadow of the former tireless dynamo I'd known. In the summer evenings I'd help her into her favourite lounge chair where she'd inhale the scent of her beautiful flowers.

I built a woodwork archway over the central pathway and trained her roses and ivy to grow up over it. By that time, I was a teenager and proud of all the praise she lavished on me for my efforts. One day, we had three or four elderly female friends visiting, and Nana invited them to view the new construction.

"Come and see Blair's erection in the garden," she said. There was a stunned silence and I turned crimson and darn near died. Nana had a little smile on her face, and to this day, I wonder if her words were an intentional double 'entendre' to spice things up a bit.

As Nana's rheumatoid arthritis worsened, she became totally bedridden. Through it all, Nana smiled, laughed and showed us forbearance beyond belief. Coming in off the school bus as a sixteen year old, my first stop was to go and see Nana for half an hour. A typical teenager, I'd shudder as I made the twenty steps down the hallway to her bedroom. Nana would perk up, smile, and ask me how my day had been, who I had seen, what I had done and how much fun had it proved to be. I'd try to conjure up something novel to say but soon I'd run out of exciting things to lie about.

Eventually, sitting carefully on the edge of the bed, I'd ask about her day. I think I learned to do a guarded eye-roll in anticipation of what she could possibly find to narrate that was worth hearing.

But Nana was Nana. As soon as I'd ask she'd start describing her day. Initially, I'd only half listen to her monologue, then, always unexpectedly, I'd find myself getting engrossed in her renditions of the world as she saw it.

"Well, I didn't really sleep last night, but its just amazing what you can remember when you've got the time to think. Do you remember when…..?" she'd start, and before I knew it, we were both back chasing squirrels, catching tadpoles, and boarding the steam train at the station.

Somewhere, back in the mists of time, Nana had escaped Grandpa's almost fanatical connection to the Kirk. She had survived witnessing his obsessive, one-hour daily Bible reading as his entrapped four offspring sat cross-legged on the kitchen floor. In my time, I can't recall her ever attending a church service. I suspect her cup had overflowed with enforced religion. So it was with some surprise that the summary of her bedridden day often included an account of what she had fathomed from reading her Bible. She'd grasp the great book, peer through her huge magnifying glass at it and start off. "I was just reading about that poor fellow Job. My, he had a hard life. Everything he tried seemed to go bad for him. No wonder people talk about the patience of Job."

She'd pause for a bit, to organize her thoughts before proffering her next gems of wisdom for my exclusive edification. As I sat there, I realized that in front of me was the personification of patience. Through her long suffering, she was uncomplaining about her lot in life, and always had that irrepressible hint of a smile on her wrinkled face.

Nana had shrunk down to a shadow of her younger, spunky, vigorous self. I doubt if she was ever over a hundred pounds even in her prime, but near the end of her life, she was a tiny, wounded sparrow still trying to fly.

She was a fighter, and latterly tried every imaginable 'cure' for her ailments. There had never been alcohol in the house but mysteriously there appeared a quarter bottle of Glenlivet whiskey. This 'medicine', mixed into a toddy, with one sugar cube on a spoon, would cause the lovely old lady to pucker up into horrendous contortions, with accompanying outlandish shrieks, as she forced down the demon potion. On other occasions, there was equally calamitous imbibing of 'curative' Guinness beer. Nana took all of a spoonful of the murky fluid with abject disgust. Tiny bottles of Drambuie, Baileys, Brandy and even Saki eventually found their way to her bedside table. The 'pharmacopeia' of items tried, also ran the gamut of hot water bottles, ice packs, poultices, copper bangles, magnets, herbs, spices and other failures.

An unforgettable foray into last-ditch efforts was the venture into apitherapy. I was dispatched, jar in hand, into the garden to catch a honeybee. There must have been a thousand of them gathering their nectar from the flowers that sunny day but it took ages to finally capture one of the busy little creatures in the jar. Then, as Nana had read in some reliable pamphlet, the trick was to place the open end of the container over her swollen knee and have the poor little prisoner sting her and so release the guaranteed therapeutic venom.

As everybody knows, bees sting even when seemingly unprovoked. However, trying to get this bee to perform this service on demand proved hopeless. Nana shrieked in pain as we wobbled her skeletally thin leg with the jar clamped onto the knee trying to activate the noncompliant aviator. Eventually, the irate prisoner escaped and wreaked retribution with a kamikaze plunge into my neck. I hadn't seen Nana so entertained for ages. That incident was a conversational topic for months and each time brought out great therapeutic happiness. "I'm so sorry that happened!" she'd say, before convulsing into laughter.

After I left home and joined the army, my visits were rather infrequent but I'd always spend quality time at her bedside, trying to repay a few of the thousands of hours she'd given me, along with the priceless gifts of wisdom and laughter and love.

The sad time came when I had to say goodbye prior to my departure for three years in Malaya. We'd decided as a family that I'd just say I was leaving and might be away for a while longer this time. She was eighty and it was almost certain to be the last time I'd see her. I choked back the tears, as it hurt so much to look her in the eye and tell a lie. I hugged her so very gently and tried not to bolt for the door. She stopped me one step from escape, "You'll be just fine, Blair," she said, "Enjoy yourself."

I stumbled up the corridor and got my luggage ready at the front door. Uncle Bill, who was leaving on the same midnight train, went down to the bedroom to say his goodbyes. We were surprised at the brevity of his visit to the bedroom but his face told me instantly that Nana had given me her last cheery words, her last gift of a farewell smile and a hug.

I managed to extend my embarkation leave for three more days to attend Nana's funeral and burial in the century old Farish family plot. That was my last gift to Nana.

A Hard Act to Follow

*A*fter my grandmother's passing, I recognized belatedly that others in my family circle had also contributed greatly to my welfare, upbringing and heritage. To some degree they had been shut out by a veil of secrecy that I'd been sheltered behind.

It may be difficult for today's modern readers to even imagine the attitudes in the late 1930's in that rural setting. Grandfather, a long time elder of the rigid and radically unforgiving Kirk, was almost maniacal at the news of his unwed daughter's pregnant status. His desolation and anger were evident in the recently unearthed news of a hellish outburst when he almost came to blows with a fellow tradesman. That colleague had had the audacity and temerity to say, "I hear yer dochters ganna have a surprise wee one."

It was a bygone era, so very far from the twenty-first century, where marriage has become a frequently declined option rather than a necessity in similar circumstances. Banishment, before the bump became evident was the edict that was brought on by the head of the household in those earlier days. It was possibly his well-meaning way of salvaging both the family's and his daughter's good name in the community.

The details of that tragic exile, my birth and subsequent handing over to a kind, welcoming couple, unknown and unrelated to our family, are matters that have now gone to the grave. So too are the details of how I was returned to my real family.

Sometime after my grandfather suffered a massive stroke and his subsequent death, Nana traveled to Ayr and brought me home. I have the greatest admiration for my mother's courage during those lost years and her well-hidden sorrow that continued while she perpetuated the myth that kept her from proudly acknowledging me as her son.

Struggling with the sensitivity and discomfort created by my mother's unmarried status, on my arrival in the family home at about age four, it was established that my mother and three uncles would be addressed by first name: Maimie, Joe, Dick and Bill. This form of address was a further attempt to keep the secret of my actual relationship in the family from the community, and from me. It was only on the eve of my departure to the army eighteen years later that the truth of my relationship was finally revealed. For my mother, a moment of tears and guilt at the painful secrecy, for me it was a time of anger and sadness after the dark years of wondering.

Only very recently, I became aware that news of my birth had actually been heralded on that 1938 occasion, by the local announcer of all worthwhile information and gossip, the milkman, who delivered to each house every day. Amazingly, perhaps out of sympathy and respect for the family, I never heard a murmur of this news from any of the villagers or school pupils.

When Nana died it must have been a tough assignment for my mother to take over the family reigns. Nana had been a brilliant and fearless leader. She would have been proud of how well her daughter succeeded her.

Maimie was the original multi-tasker. For years, as the sole breadwinner in the family home, she juggled half a dozen part-time jobs and still found time to be chief cook and bottle washer, house cleaner and nurse to the sick.

Two days per week, she would run up the hill to the village to catch the 9:15 am bus that took her miles up the glen. There she was executive secretary and bookkeeper for a huge farming company. She'd return on the 7:00 pm bus to embark on her second career, managing our household. A discrete little plaque near the front door announced her third calling. Like her father before her, she was the Registrar of Births, Deaths, and Marriages for the District. As in so many home-based businesses, all the recording and documentation, and discussion of these matters with clients, occurred on and around the big kitchen table in the only heated room in the house. There, as a silent observer, I learned about the need for confidentiality and accuracy of detail that that work necessitated.

From that environment, I also learned the art of evasion and the telling of 'wee white lies', as necessary mistruths were then called. I recall an occasion when a ten year old school friend said, "Oh, I saw Jessie and her man go into your hoose last night. Are they getting married?"

"I don't know," I lied. "There was talk of gardening and fishing and fitba." It was good training if I'd wanted to become a spy.

Maimie was also a sales agent for the Alliance Insurance Company, secretary treasurer for the local Squire (Landowner), shorthand recorder and typist for various organizations, and treasurer for the Wee Free Kirk. To fill any interludes she had frequent verbal battles with her twin brother Dick as she tried to decipher the scrawled documentation of his business accounts and payments as the last of the original family joiners and undertakers. Exasperation was peaked occasionally as the written confirmation of some financial transaction over the building of a farmer's hayshed appeared in the form of scribbled numbers on a piece of 2"x4" scrap lumber.

It was in the days before the onset of conflict of interest. No mention was ever made of the connection of overlapping duties involved in Dick's undertaker/coffin- making segments of his career and Maimie's registration requirement of documentation of deaths.

Another sideline that brought in a few shillings to the family coffers was one that was a sign of the times in the immediate post-war years of poverty. Maimie organized and ran the Littlewood's Home Shopping Club. This was a popular working class program, described as 'buying on the never, never', a precursor to today's buy now, pay later schemes. From a huge book much like today's Sears Catalogue, a group of fifteen to twenty local residents and neighbours would select an item they wished to purchase but couldn't afford at that time. Often it was an item of clothing or occasionally something as extravagant as a child's pram, or in modern vernacular, a stroller.

The system entailed making a payment of one-twentieth of the cost price per week, till the full payment was complete. A draw was made each week to see who would get their selected item that week. It made for a lot of knocking on doors and the proffering of one shilling and eleven pence or whatever was the weekly payment by that individual. These moments were interesting social and business transactions and taught me much of my ability to chat with anybody I meet. They also helped improve my skill in one of the three R's, arithmetic. Today, thanks to that background, I can still mentally add up the cost of a few groceries faster than some supermarket cashiers with their calculators.

In summer, I'd be dispatched to the riverbank and woodlands to pick wild raspberries and blackberries. These Maimie would craft into delicious jams and jellies to add to the selection of others made from rhubarb, gooseberry, red currant and honey. Samples of that merchandise just happened to be located on the windowsill and available for sale to our many visitors.

When I was sixteen, Maimie married Alex Spence, a local farmer, after a few years of quiet courtship. He was a widower with two children, Roy and Margaret, who were eighteen and fifteen at the time. The wedding, in the Craig Kirk, was a very private ceremony.

Aside from the officiating minister, Maimie's twin brother Dick, and her cousin Tib were the only attendees. I got news of the event from Uncle Joe when I came off the school bus that evening, the bride and groom having gone off for a three-day honeymoon.

Maimie's already busy life shot into even greater multi-tasking mode as she now commuted between Broombush and her new home on the farm. She still cooked and cared for Nana, an ailing Uncle Joe, and myself at Broombush, while also taking on the farm household chores and married life. Regrettably, at the time, I still wasn't aware that she was my mother, so I didn't identify Alex as a stepfather nor his children as step-siblings, and I never lived on the farm. I continued to live at Broombush, aside from when I stayed in Dumfries while working for the Post Office, until I left for the army. Alex died in 1970 and shortly thereafter Maimie moved off the farm to a house on a small acreage that had been planned as their retirement home.

I visited Margaret on my marathon journey through Australia in 1963. She died there in 1990. I keep in contact with Roy and his family. We visit when we are in Scotland, and I hosted him and his wife here in Cranbrook a few years ago.

In her youth, Maimie had been an outstanding badminton player. Every community had its club in the village hall. It was one of the very few inexpensive sports and leisure-time activities that were within the reach of her social group. I learned early in life that she could out-match me with ease, but she was perceptive enough to pretend to miss enough shots to allow me to win on lots of occasions.

Returning from three years in Malaya in 1964, where I'd played competitively almost every day, I mentioned that I was going to the village hall to have a game. She said, "Oh, I haven't played for years; that would be fun." That hadn't exactly been an invitation on my part. I was hoping to go out and perhaps impress my counterparts (female, no doubt) with my newly acquired improved skills at the game.

Seeing the crowds on the courts, she said, "Maybe I'll just have a wee game with you and then leave and let you have fun on your own." That conflicted with my planned agenda but I knew better than to mention her old age to my fifty-one year old mother. Let's just say that I lost decisively and exited the building with mother rather than face the subsequent disdain of the younger set.

For my last five years in the army, weekly letters exchanged with Maimie continued the learning, encouragement, and nurturing. She kept my gradually worsening, illegible scrawls tied in tidy bundles that I found in the attic thirty years later, testament to the close connection and love we had shared.

She visited Canada twenty times in her last two decades. Maimie had many of my Nana's attributes and my sons, Ian and Craig, remember her as their beloved Nana. Diminutive in stature, dynamo by nature, she was pretty, had a vivacious smile, a wicked sense of humour and boundless energy all genetically handed down. As Nana to my sons, she was that same wonderful gift to them that her mother had been to me.

One of her passions, during those holidays, was to attend the local Stock Car Racing. She'd get very excited and would yell out her over-enthusiastic support for her favourite driver and car. At times, I was quite embarrassed by her utterances but the mostly young spectators would be quite taken by the little old grey haired lady with the loud voice. Craig and Ian loved it when their Nana got so excited.

Another surprising contradiction I had to cope with as she aged brought about many a friendly discussion between us. As a teenager I'd been firmly admonished against the depravity of visiting the billiard hall in town. It was a place of questionable moral uprightness, being a location where smoking, drinking and betting occurred, and it was also the hang-out for scantily dressed young women. I recall that it was the first place where I saw a tattoo on a woman's, let's say, shoulder.

In her seventies, Maimie became a TV Snooker aficionado and she even phoned from Scotland just to tell me that Steven Hendry, the reigning world champion, a Scot of course, had just achieved the maximum break possible of one hundred forty-seven. I had no idea what that meant, but her enthusiasm made it an indisputable fact, although I did later Google it just to check.

Also in her seventies, she took up curling and became just as enthusiastic about her involvement in that new sport as she was with all other life challenges. I only watched her on the ice once, and shook my head at the vigor she put into sweeping, comparative to players half her age.

She finally began driving a car at age seventy. She had obtained a license during the war when authorities were desperate to find drivers for ambulances and simply gave out the document without a test. Although she had never been behind the wheel of a car she consistently renewed her license every few years, just in case. At seventy she decided it was time.

I can't say I taught her to drive, but I did go out with her as a white-knuckled passenger on her first few ventures over the moors. It didn't take long for the sheep and highland cattle to give way to the noisy little Volkswagen Polo as Maimie gradually overcame the incompatibility of clutch and gearshift. Eventually, her driving style evolved showing signs of her competitive nature and memories of her Stock Car racing spectator experiences.

Even years later, on the occasion when she had driven sixty miles to meet me at Prestwick for my annual short visit to Scotland, my overnight flight jet lag vanished in the first five miles of her driving. Pleading carsickness that I only experienced as a passenger, I convinced Maimie to give me the wheel. She wasn't impressed as I nodded my way to Dumfries.

When I heard the sad news of her death in a road accident at age eighty, the hurt was lessened slightly by the knowledge that she had been driving herself to the curling club when she crashed into one of the country road dry stone walls. Remembering the long drawn out years of pain my Nana had suffered, I'm sure Maimie would have been relieved that her death was not prolonged with suffering. She was a great admirer of Robert Burns and her sudden demise fit so well with his line:

"Like the snowflake on the river, one moment there, then gone forever."

I've learned much from her love, teachings and support over the years and have inherited many of her traits of athletic competitiveness, humour and kindness to others. She set such high standards in so many facets of life, as did her mother, that Maimie too, is a hard act to follow.

The Three Uncles

*S*ingle parent families survive many circumstances, happenings and consequences that are often incomprehensible for those who haven't been in that segment of society. Being without a father in the home was my lot, but I had the great good fortune to have three uncles who tried to out do each other in their efforts to nurture, love and guide me as a child. Belatedly, I realise that, with these three wise men in my life I can now look back and almost say, "Who needed a father?"

My uncles, Joe, Bill and Dick had immense influence in my upbringing, and contributed equally in shaping who I am today. The diversity of their individual characters, knowledge, skills, and expertise covered a spectrum that no one man could have offered.

The oldest of the family, Uncle Joe, was born in 1907. He had the good fortune to excel academically and stayed at school till he was seventeen, an uncommon happening back when many left school at twelve or thirteen. He was also an artist. I'm pleased to still have some of his pencil sketches and art work from his early teenage years. Those won prizes and were early indicators of his aptitude and attention to detail which would lead him into draftsmanship and architecture.

During the war he was employed in some hush-hush secretive work in an ammunition and weapons manufacturing centre forty miles from our home. As with so many others, throughout his entire life, he never did divulge the nature of that work.

Chronic ill health brought him permanently back to the family home by the time I was twelve. I immediately benefited from his interest in meteorology. A wind vein on the roof connected to a surplus aircraft instrument dial showed the prevailing wind direction. His 'piece-de-resistance' was a hygrometer that he fashioned out of some other cockpit instrument. It measured the humidity using the shortening and lengthening of a strand of my mother's hair as its detecting mechanism. I keenly observed his meticulous chronicling of rainfall, wind speed and humidity in his impeccable calligraphy, but unfortunately did not inherit that skill.

In his little locked shed behind the house everything was in its place in row upon row of carefully named and stacked boxes containing screws, nails, bolts and gadgets. Every chisel, hammer and screwdriver was clipped in its designated place in the cupboard. I had the privilege of being allowed into his little workshop but woe-betide me if I borrowed anything and failed to replace it. Despite his patient, tranquil nature, I do recall an incident when an unexpected explosive side of his character erupted. That I am here to tell the tale is truly a miracle, and explains his hysterical reaction. At age eight I tested an electrical socket using two bent nails -- 240-volt circuits can be fatal! I was banned from his shed for weeks after that experiment.

Joe took the time to explain everything in his world to me and I look back in awe at the diversity of his interests. Without his guidance, algebra and calculus would have been 'Greek' to me. By example, he made me inquisitive and hungry for knowledge. His shyness and reclusive nature also rubbed off on me as a boy. Gentle and kind, his regular attendance at the Wee Free Kirk of Scotland was on a last-in first-out basis due to his almost anti-social reserve, yet he could recite each sermon almost verbatim. Above all, he taught me to be uncomplaining about personal health problems, and tolerant of life's challenges.

A railway station master in a tiny village in bleak Galloway, Uncle Bill was the smart dresser of the three brothers. On a visit to me in Cranbrook in his mid-seventies, helping me split fire wood, he showed up to work in a long-sleeved dress shirt (handkerchief tucked in the wristband), collar, tie, Trilby hat, and a pipe that produced hostile St. Bruno fumes.

Extroverted, but a caring individual, Bill could converse comfortably with tramp or aristocrat. Going to church and gardening were his delights, but his great passion was amateur dramatics which many Scottish villages hosted and toured to neighbouring halls. Much of my humour echoes his constant wit. I also learned about acceptance, and not being too judgemental from him. His son, Neilson, and I were nearer brothers than cousins and spent summer, Easter and Christmas holidays around our country home. Bill, a staunch teetotaller, showed his understanding and forgiving nature when he supported Neilson's choice to become a pub owner, a career that lasted thirty years. In the latter years of my Nana's life, Bill spent an enormous amount of time visiting her in her terminal state, and taught me the compassion and caring I have for the sick and needy today.

Happy-go-lucky would describe the youngest of the three brothers. Uncle Dick had been obliged to follow in my grandfather's footsteps as an apprentice carpenter at age fourteen. My mother's twin, he too was involved in the village drama club and usually was selected for the role of the comedy actor in the annual productions.

Like so many young men at that time, he went off to war (and fortunately came back safely) but would never talk about anything that had happened there. He was a plump man and once I cheekily observed that he looked slim in an old army snap-shot taken in Milan.

"Aye, you'd be slim too, if you'd hauled a machine gun all the way up the length of Italy."

As a youngster I often accompanied him on trips in his capacity as undertaker. He'd take me along to open and close gates as we travelled to some distant shepherd's cottage, miles over the moors. I'd sit in the car while he measured the body before returning to the workshop to make the coffin. Macabre as it may seem, he had an endless supply of stories about that side of his profession. I recall imploring him to repeat some of them as we drove along.

"Tell me that story again about the coffin falling off the trailer at midnight."

He'd embellish the facts yet again and I'd shriek with laughter. "It's a serious business," he'd always insist, engendering more gales of laughter. I suspect I've inherited his embellishing gene.

When I was about age ten Uncle Dick began to take me along to help with his painting and decorator work. Those were the days when great flower-patterned wall-paper was in vogue. My job was to get the flour paste brushed onto the long rolls of paper. Some of the sheets needed on staircase walls were sixteen feet long, so it was a two-man, or man and wee boy, job to transport the paper up the ceiling-high ladders. Of course each new strip had to match or correspond with the previous patterned piece. Occasionally a three-inch gap would be left at the top so I'd be ordered to supply a spare piece to fill the gap. "Big red flower on the left," would be the request, so I'd send up, on a pole, my guess of the appropriate flowery filler patch. It was years later that I found out I have a serious colour discrimination deficit. Hence, his constant remark, "It's the wrong colour, but it will never be seen in the dark."

He could make anybody laugh and brought the serious competitiveness of friendly games of cards into riotous party atmosphere. "Oh, you can't play that card," he'd interject, straight-faced, challenging the opponent.

"Why not," the player would demand on the edge of anger.

"Because I cannot beat it," Dick would reply, sending the place into howls of laughter.

Being introduced by an acquaintance to someone he'd never met, he once stated, "Oh, it's a pleasure for you to meet me," bringing instant levity when the penny dropped.

He passed away at age ninety-two, enjoying life to the end. I still phone his widow, Aunt Jean, each Sunday. We conjure up one or two great memories of Dick, a husband, father, uncle, friend, comedian, teacher and fine example of how to live life to the full.

I'm grateful for the example, direction and love those three wonderful men showered on me and hope to pass these gifts on to my children, step-children and grandchildren. Instead of the three bears' story, I hope the wee ones will remember the wisdom and laughter of the three uncles.

Broombush

*T*he old family home nestled on the banks of the River Cairn has changed very little in structure since it was built in 1904. Of course well constructed granite, sandstone and slate- roofed homesteads were meant to stand the test of time, evidenced by some of the thousand year old castles and ancestral homes still prominent in the glens and hill tops and islands of Scotland.

Broombush took its name from the profusion of brilliant yellow shrubs, known as broom, that covered the edge of the woodland overlooking the house. The front door of the house was a mere five feet from the asphalt surface of the narrow country road. Named the 'Black Brae', that steep, winding road led half a mile from our glen to the nearby village.

Dunscore, population 250, was the source of all things necessary for everyday life. It had a grocery shop; butcher; garage; church; school (capacity thirty pupils in six grades) two pubs; one country doctor's house with one examining room and one tiny waiting room; hotel with three rooms to let; village hall; carpenter's shop; and hearse house. Being that close to such an array of amenities, Broombush was as near to Utopia as a wee boy could hope for.

I was oblivious to any shortcomings in the house. Life there seemed normal, and was comfortable despite what today might seem like serious short-comings. There was an out-house toilet, a warm kitchen (the only heated room in the place) and simple food. All cooking was done on the log and coal-fuelled kitchen fireplace. To me, it was just perfect because the people there made that house a wonderful home.

Broombush even had the newest, most exciting advances in technology and services that emerged in the late 30's. The phone number, Dunscore 29, told that we were on the leading edge of scientific advancement. Furthermore, running water had been recently installed via the modern miracle of lead piping from a reservoir miles up in the hills. To cap even those break-throughs, electricity arrived in 1938.

As a bonus, Broombush was located in a magical playground that offered an abundance of adventure. The river was a year round source of pleasure and excitement. Placid in summer and only knee-deep near the house, it had a large eight-foot deep pool just a hundred yards upstream. There, you could see fifteen-pound salmon lazily lying in the depths of what was the village swimming hole. Downstream, past the wide, single-span, sandstone and granite road bridge, whose scaffolding had been erected by my carpenter forbearers in 1818, the river fell into a cascading boulder-strewn gulch. The Linn, as it was called, was a treacherous mile that lured youngsters like a magnet.

During the summers, my cousin Neilson was my playmate for the entire school holidays. We built a raft from rough fencing boards salvaged from the flotsam that came down the river in the flood time. Strapped to six empty, five-gallon oil drums, this framework held us, mostly, above water level as we poled our way upstream for a mile or so then drifted back down having fun in the lazy hazy days of summer.

Late September would bring the advent of torrential rain storms, which turned the tranquil river into a raging flood, sweeping over its banks. That was when the Cairn River held its greatest appeal for us as teenagers. Massive beech trees lined the banks near home and lured the daredevils to devise the ultimate challenge. Some of these tree branches, six inches thick where they left the main trunk, spread out forty feet across the swirling brown waters. The dare was to crawl out on the branches till the climber's weight bent them down enough that he could touch the water. Scary stuff, but so exciting.

The same trees offered yet another source of fun. Neilson and I sewed up some borrowed/stolen burlap potato sacks and made them into a hammock that we stretched from the trees fifty feet above the raging river. How we survived still makes me shudder sixty years later.

The woods just fifty yards from the front door of Broombush were also a great place to play. Small rock outcrops were our eight-foot high precipices to scale, and the treed area was a hide-and-seek heaven for ten year olds. There was also an abandoned and only partially filled-in trench in those woods. It had been the site of a war time observation post used by the Home Guard. Those stalwart old soldiers, some of them Boer War and World War One veterans, had manned that bunker during the nights in the early 1940's, keeping up their vigil lest the enemy infiltrate that peaceful corner of the country. My three or four cronies and I unleashed greater imaginary firepower from that trench than had ever been the case in reality. The locals, out for their Sunday afternoon stroll, would have been horrified if they'd realised they were in the wooden gun sights of new young defenders in the early 1950's.

Wet days, of which there are many in Scotland, found Neilson and I in the Broombush attic. It was a place of mice and spider webs and dust, but also a depository of unimaginable treasures. There was a glass-covered display case containing dozens of eggs of different bird species. Of course we had been told to never touch those precious items, so we handled them with great care. We were in awe of the varieties of colours, shapes and sizes, from huge swan eggs to those of the tiny wren. Other treasures ran the gamut from ancient violins, accordions, a grandfather clock, paintings of severe old great-great-grandparents, wooden homemade toy trucks, and figure skates from an earlier era, to huge family Bibles and other vintage, musty books. (Today these items might bring a tidy sum on EBay.) When our absence was finally noticed we'd be cajoled to come down the rickety access ladder. Asked if we'd seen anything interesting during our stay aloft we'd usually answer, "No, nothing new," unaware of the play on words we'd inadvertently voiced.

As a young teenager I began to realise that I had a significant part to play in the team work that was needed to keep things solvent at Broombush. I never thought to complain as I pitched in to help alleviate the poverty of those post war days. Much earlier, at the age of seven, I brought home my first two trout, small, but enough to feed Nana, my mother and myself for supper. That contribution to the lean food supply of the times was one of my earliest experiences of pride in accomplishment. Fishing was a pastime sport of my youth, but it also provided an important source of food for the family. Vegetable gardening too was my responsibility so potatoes, cabbage, turnips and carrots were all part of the day's work. A further source of food came free, snaring the abundant wild rabbit population

The family purchased coal for that one kitchen fire, but there was sparing use made of that expensive fuel. My major job was to bring in cut and chopped firewood from all available free sources. There seemed to be an ongoing supply of deadfall in the nearby woods which could be harvested with a trusty handsaw. I can't ever recall seeing a chainsaw till I came to Canada.

The river too was a source of sticks, branches and even logs swept down in the floods. Fashioning a large three-point hook attached to a length of rope solved the problem of retrieving these floating supplies of firewood. With the other end of the rope attached to a healthy tree on the river bank I'd throw the catcher hook over a passing branch and let the fast current swing the trapped lumber into the bank. These were then cut into manageable lengths and stacked on land, where they could dry off for use months later.

Broombush, over the years of my youth was a place where I was pampered and loved, but also turned out to be a place of great learning opportunities. These diverse skills have paid off immensely in my adult life. I like to think I've passed on much of this knowledge to the next generation.

A recent visit to Broombush in the company of my two adult sons, Ian and Craig, brought back many fond memories as we were shown through that beautifully renovated home by the present owners. The attic, without spiders, is now a gorgeous bedroom. Other new additions include a dining room, a study, a sitting room and plans for a future attached solarium overlooking the garden. The twenty-first century has also brought in the long awaited two and a half bathrooms, although I credit my speed over fifty yards to the bygone midnight rain-swept dashes to the old outhouse. The garden is now worthy of inclusion in a rural horticulture and flower show tour. The same lupins, gladioli, and peony roses that brought such joy to my Nana still bring beauty and scents to stir my memory.

Broombush, that two hundred-fifty pound house that my grandfather built in 1904 is now worth every penny of the half million it would fetch today. I hope it brings as much happiness to the family under its roof today, as it did for me more than half a century ago.

The Miller's Tale

$\mathcal{J}$immy Little, the miller, was yet another gem of my youth who contributed in his own unique way to help nurture and guide that wee country boy to become the person I am today.

He was a tiny man, just over five feet tall, his build at odds with the heavy, physical labour of his life's work. What he lacked in stature he more than made up for in boundless energy. Ancient and well worn, or so his sixty years appeared to me, Jimmy had an irrepressible grin and faced all of his challenges with predictable good humour and vigor.

He leased a twenty acre small-holding where he raised a few pigs, two cows and in some token sequence of rotation, planted and harvested five acres of oats, some turnips and an acre of potatoes.

He also cut, by scythe, a half-mile stretch of hay on the riverbank to supply his stock and his horse with three or four small ricks of hay.

Despite these agricultural pursuits, Jimmy was best known in our village as 'the miller'. The village grain mill was owned by the manor or 'big hoose' of the area, but it was Jimmy Little who operated it. All the local farmers brought their bagged oats to be processed at the mill, turning the raw oats into the 'bruised corn' that was then fed to their stock.

The huge water-wheel mechanism of the mill was a sight that never failed to impress onlookers. The damned-up millpond had a constant deep pool of headwater with a sluice gate which, when opened, turned the mill wheel. (The pond itself, some six feet in depth was home to numerous trout, eels and salmon, the latter of which often made their way into the creels of nighttime poachers.)

When I was about five years old, Jimmy Little adopted me as his 'helper' and introduced me to the miracle and magic of machinery. With his help, I'd engage the great lever that raised the sluice gate on the headrace water channel. This allowed the damned-up height of water to flow onto the paddles of the thirty-foot high wheel. It never failed to give me a thrill to see that massive vertical mechanism start turning. I learned that the wheel rotated on a huge axle, which in turn, using immense wooden gears, drove the top millstone. The millstone weighed one ton but the wheel, creating five-horse power of energy made this amazing event take place.

Inside the mill, gadgetry enabled Jimmy to hoist huge bags of grain up from one floor of the mill to the next, through a trap door, by a simple pull on a rope. The grain would then be lugged into the drying kiln and spread across its tinned flooring. I helped throw the occasional log into the kiln fire below while the miller did the heavy lifting. We were a great team.

I was never allowed into the kiln itself, but the maestro would disappear into that dark, smoke-filled sanctum to turn the oats by hand. He'd reappear, fifteen minutes later, drenched in sweat, coughing as if it was his last gasp. Ironically, his relief from that oxygen-starved chamber was to move outside to the front-loading bench and light up his favourite pipe stoked with foul-smelling

St. Bruno tobacco. There he would take time to tell me stories or explain the workings of the mill. His own children were grown and had left home. I provided pleasant companionship for him in that solitary, noisy environment, and for me it was a thrilling adventure each time I visited.

Farmers who brought in their cartloads of grain, paid on a per bag basis for the milling. Frequently there was some dispute on the quantity of finished product returned to them to use as cattle feed. I was always ushered off until these altercations were concluded. Even from a distance I could tell that the vocabulary was what we now describe as 'unprintable'.

Jimmy's farming pursuits were a diversion that he enjoyed, and as I got a little older I made token contributions to each aspect of that homestead's productivity. There I learned to milk his two cows, although the half-hour it took me to milk each beast compared to Jimmy's ten minute operation, was not appreciated by the cows. In consequence there were many half-filled pails kicked away during my milking apprenticeship. Working with Jimmy I developed a deep appreciation of the "sweat of the brow' needed on that small farm. Planting and harvesting the potatoes was back-breaking toil, and the memory of shawing frost-encrusted turnips on a frigid October morning still makes me shudder.

Jimmy's' one old horse, Billy, was the beast of burden, source of all the heavy work of ploughing, raking, furrowing and loosening the crop ready for hand-picking. Likewise the three or four small stacks of hay were hand-loaded onto Billy's cart and transported to the little hayshed near the mill.

Billy was a gentle old animal and I have fond memories of him. I recall being hoisted onto his broad back at the tender age of eight for a momentous adventure. He was a mountain of a beast viewed from that height, and it was bareback riding at its most frightening, as carthorses did not have saddles or stirrups.

My excursion was to travel the four miles to the nearest blacksmith to have Billy re-shod. The outward journey was completed in about an hour or so at a steady plod. Arriving at the smithy, Billy sensed the other horses and the smell of singed hooves where the hot new shoes had been seared onto the animals' feet. The blacksmith came to my rescue, lifted me down from my perch and took the reluctant Billy into the yard. I watched in horror as the old shoes were removed, the feet trimmed and filed, then the still-hot shoes nailed on. At the end of the procedure, Billy was a bit skittish and didn't take well to me being on his back. Once we headed home, however, he soon settled down, tolerated my presence, and needed no real guidance as he knew the way.

About a mile from home, I spotted a particularly lush clump of grass near the stonewall edging the road. I steered Billy up close to that wall and slid off onto the convenient dismount helper of the three-foot high dyke. Billy took his time gorging on the offered lunch. I then had an unanticipated problem. When I tried to coax Billy back to stand beside the wall to facilitate remounting he wouldn't side-up to the dyke. On the final long mile home I was sometimes leading him, more often he was dragging me, but never was I riding. Although I didn't meet anyone on that lonely road, the story was around the community like wildfire, and, worst of all, was the joke of the school on my arrival next morning.

Billy and Jimmy's relationship had another well-know feature. Jimmy leased a small field some two miles from the mill where he'd crop hay or turnips in season. After an exhausting day of haymaking, horse and master would turn towards home in the evening. Especially in the heat of summer, at the crossroads half a mile from the mill, Jimmy would steer horse and cart homewards. Jimmy then ventured off to the village pub to recuperate. Billy would make his way home along the narrow country road, negotiating right of way with other traffic, even occasionally the evening double-decker bus. Arriving home he would tuck in to the haystack and munch away contentedly. Three pints later, Jimmy would wend his way home, often in full song, oblivious to the almost predictable scolding welcome from his long suffering wife, Bella.

I think Robert Burns' description of such occasions fits the bill. Similarly inebriated on his return from a local hostelry, Burns pondered the home-coming welcome awaiting him: "Where sits his sulken, sullen dame, nursing her wrath to keep it warm."

Jimmy's other weakness was a fondness for rather more speedy equestrian species than Billy. By Saturday morning he'd have studied the form of that day's horse races and was ready with his bets. As a regular contributor, very occasional winner, he had good standing with the betting shops in town. He didn't have a phone in his little farm house so would appear at our kitchen door, rather cap-in-hand, and request the use of our phone to place his bets.

He'd first step up to the fireplace and place the appropriate payment on the mantelpiece, taking change as needed from the assorted coins that lay there, the 'phone money' as it was called. All this was transacted on the honour system. He'd then tiptoe down the corridor to where the phone hung on the wall, and dial the operator to connect his call to place the bets for the 2:30, 3 o'clock and 3:30 races.

By the time he'd return, my Nana would have the kettle on the fire for the cup of tea and chat that ensued. The gossip and pleasantries would fill in the next half hour.

Despite the heat, dust and noise of the mill, and the heavy labour involved in his agricultural tasks, time with Jimmy was a comfort for me. He had an unending repertoire of stories, and he taught me many practical skills. Most of all, he was my friend, and I have many fond memories of my times with him.

Mrs. Lawrie

Old Mrs. Lawrie was another of the wonderful people I had the good fortune to encounter as a youngster. Her little cottage was part of the loose cluster of homes whose occupants were described as the 'Brig end folks'. This nomenclature derived from their picturesque setting on the banks of the River Cairn close to Dalgonar Bridge, at one time described as the widest single span bridge in Scotland.

My connection with Mrs. Lawrie was through the mutually beneficial neighborliness so common in rural hamlets in Scotland in those days. A widow of some years, she had migrated from an isolated shepherd's cottage on the moors to the relative metropolis of the half dozen cottages, only half a mile from the village of Dunscore. She was part of the country 'come on in' clan who thrived on regular visits from neighbours and friends to help pass the time of day. My diverse activities and connections through school, delivering papers, scout meetings, and a natural 'gift of the gab' made me a welcome visitor. I brought her the local news. It wasn't gossip; it was just relaying rumour with occasional embellishment if the subject matter was marginally mundane.

In trade for my cheery chat, Mrs. Lawrie had a seemingly endless supply of Penguin chocolate biscuits. She knew my weakness for this delicacy and would play the stalling act of setting down my cup of Ovaltine first, then searching in several biscuit tins on the mantelpiece for the much-anticipated treat. Occasionally, a twinkle in her eye, she'd say, "Oh, it's lean times, Blair, you'll maybe have to settle for shortbread today." At the disappointed look on my face she'd rock back and forth in laughter before offering the magic chocolate from her apron pocket.

Early on in my visitations, as a six year old, she'd pressed a penny in my hand for bringing in a few kindlers for fire starting. I'd scampered home proud as punch to proclaim her generosity and the fortune I'd acquired. My Nana sat me on her knee that day and gently taught me that some things should be gifts from the heart for those in need, rather than jobs done with the expectation of reward. From that day I established with Mrs. Lawrie that there was no need for recompense; but she knew a small boy would always welcome a chocolate biscuit.

I can't recall her every asking for help, but I'd say, "I'll just bring in a bucket of coals and a few sticks from the shed."

Her predictable refrain would be, "Oh you don't need to do that!"

We'd sit and chat by the fireside, my presence a comfort to her, and her stories of yesteryear entertainment and information for me. Where else would I have learned about feeding orphan lambs from a bottle; how the sheep dog Tam found the lad with the broken leg in the blizzard of '23; how Wullie, her husband had walked seven miles in the middle of the night to the nearest phone to call the doctor to help with the breach birth of their daughter, Jessie; how they'd watched their seventeen year old son go off to fight the Boche in 1917, never to return. Despite the tales of difficulty and tragedy there were a thousand stories of laughter and joy. Her face told its own story. Dominating the wrinkles of age were smile lines, evidence that happiness had outweighed grief in her four score years.

Over the years, even as a teenager, my visits to Mrs. Lawrie continued, albeit diminishing to once a week. I know she greatly appreciated the knock on the door and the 'only-in-the-country' habit of letting oneself in, calling, "It's just me again." We'd sit and chat and munch biscuits for twenty minutes or so till she'd admonish me for overstaying my welcome.

"You should be out there chasing the lasses, not sittin' here blethering with an auld womin."

Eventually I went away to the army. Only years later I wondered if she had anguished about my departure, recalling her own son's one-way journey to far off lands.

I'd find time to pay a visit to my old friend when I'd come home on leave. She'd be enthralled as I related my stories. Of course, a captive audience is target for exaggeration and embellishment when there is no opportunity to validate or dispute the facts presented by the storyteller. Looking back, I'm sure my exploits and adventures became larger in every dimension when I was describing them to her.

She was very interested in my physiotherapy training in the Military Hospital in London and she just couldn't believe that I could afford to buy a Vespa Scooter. This was not surprising, bearing in mind that she and her husband had never owned any vehicle. As I described riding over London Bridge and past Buckingham Palace she'd relate to those experiences by saying, "Oh aye, I saw pictures of those places in the paper."

Proudly, I'd regale her with accounts of my sports pursuits, especially my passion for football. Her eyes brightened up as I told of attending a cup match at Wembley where eighty thousand spectators crammed into Britain's biggest stadium. I explained that of those, seventy-five thousand had to stand to watch the game as only five thousand seats were available for those rich enough to afford the luxury of sitting.

I went on to describe my excitement about the training hospital in Woolwich. She cut me off, bright as a button, "Oh Woolwich, that's where that Arsenal side comes from." She knew the connection of that first division football club to that location because her husband, Wullie, used to mention that team when he did the football pools. (A Scottish national pastime was betting on the football results.)

Often during those visits I would try to interest her in modern changes. I once enquired whether she'd ever thought of buying a television set.

"Oh, I went to somebody's home to watch the Coronation six years ago. No, that's not for me." That summed up her one, 1953, exposure to a ten-inch black and white rendition of the century's most historic moment. Her memory of what I presumed was poor reception included the comment, "It was the middle of the summer, and it looked like they had a snowstorm in London." She added, "And I hear tell that there's crime and a lot of smut showing in those programs, and those machines are terrible expensive." I got the message.

I went back to my pride in my newfound knowledge of medical matters and launched into explaining how physiotherapy could cure everything from A to Z, Alopecia to Zygomatic sinusitis. She went on busily with her knitting, rhythmically rocking back and forth by the fireside, listening but making no response.

Mrs. Lawrie's body was showing evidence of the long years of strenuous work. Hers had been a frugal lifestyle with the necessity of bringing in buckets of water from the nearby stream, the misery of the outhouse toilet at the end of the garden, and hard physical labour to put food on the table and fuel in the fireplace. Those conditions had exacted their toll on her arthritic spine and grossly swollen stiff knees.

Showing off my new diagnostic skills I said, "Mrs. Lawrie, let me tell you about a super new treatment for arthritic knees. We've got this brand new machine in our hospital called a Kromayer Lamp. It's a sophisticated, state-of-the-art apparatus that shines ultra-violet rays onto the joints. We irradiate them for thirty seconds on an area about the size of a half crown (two inch diameter). What happens is that a large blister swells up on that spot an hour after the treatment. The surface itch and irritation, just like a bad sunburn, is quite intense and it acts as a counter-irritant so that the deep arthritic pain is overshadowed by the discomfort of the blister."

I expected amazement and appreciation. Instead I was quietly put in my place.

"That's quite interesting, but it's not new," she said.

"But, Mrs. Lawrie, this technique is so new, down in London, I doubt if they've even got such advanced treatments at Dumfries Royal Infirmary." I thought that this was the ace up my sleeve, daring to diminish the internationally-renowned nearby seven hundred-bed hospital.

"I remember my granny talking about that treatment," she said. "Oh yes, they used to wrap stinging nettles round the knees to help with painful arthritis. I imagine it worked, as a- what was that you called it?-counter-irritation, wasn't it? They were pretty smart in those days, you know."

Even the grandfather clock's metronomic tick-tock smirked at me. It sounded like, "got ya!" She skillfully changed the subject with the offer of another Penguin biscuit and more anecdotes of past follies, inserting some self-deprecatory tales of her own.

Years later, I read a medical review of another 'newly' identified potential treatment for spinal arthritis. It involved circulatory stimulus. Relief of pain was achieved by exposing arthritic joints to gentle movement caused by electrical vibration in special chairs and the oscillation in waterbeds. These new methods reminded me that my old friend, Mrs. Lawrie, had instituted that same beneficial treatment for her arthritic knees and spine with the rhythmic movement in her rocking chair, at least half a century earlier. They were pretty smart in those days!

My visits to Mrs. Lawrie over many years of my childhood, as a teenager, and especially as a young man experiencing a wide new world away from home, always grounded me. She helped me, in the most subtle ways, understand that intelligence, value and beauty are often where you least expect to find them.

As a postscript, Dumfries Royal Infirmary, have recently, started plans for a one hundred twenty million pound expansion, presumably to bring the facility up to date and enable them to offer all the most modern treatments that Mrs. Lawrie and her predecessors had pioneered in years gone by.

The Boy on the Bike

Keir Village, four miles from our family home, was once a
thriving little community with its church, grocery store, blacksmith
shop, and cluster of a dozen houses nestled along the banks of the
River Cairn. Downgraded to hamlet at best, with the closure of the
store, school and gradual decay of some of the houses, it still clings
to its fame of the 1860's. The blacksmith shop at that time claimed to
have been the birthplace of the pedal bicycle. A large plaque on the
front of the now-closed and somewhat derelict building keeps vigil
over that historical site. Kirkpatrick MacMillan, blacksmith by trade
and inventor of that new miracle machine, would have had no idea
of the impact a bicycle would have in my life ninety years later.

To my utter surprise, amazement, and delight, my family bought me a new Elswick bike for my eighth birthday. I cannot even imagine where they found the money for such a costly purchase in the immediate post war years, a time of abject poverty. The rickety old family car, a 1928 Standard number ASM 687, then eighteen years old, was still moving but only just, having had a bit of a rest throughout the war years when we couldn't afford the petrol to run it. So in relative terms the new bike was an absolute extravagance.

Aware of just how fortunate I was, I treasured the gift and guarded it with my life. At first I wouldn't take the wee bike out in the rain and spent ages polishing and nurturing it as if it had been a Rolls Royce. Soon, however, it became the versatile vehicle for all my excursions and projects. I had the luxury of now cycling, instead of walking, the half mile up to the village to buy groceries, and I soon began to see the entrepreneurial opportunities afforded by my new vehicle. To begin with I developed my own newspaper delivery business. This was only to four different households but involved a two-mile journey, indicative of the wide spread of habitations in that rural setting.

By the time I was nine, I had landed the much-sought-after job of delivering telegrams. In the late 40's in rural Scotland, few houses had telephones so urgent vital communication about sickness, births or deaths came into the village post-office by phone and then was delivered to the household by typed telegram.

Our family home was one of the few in the surrounding area that had a phone. This good fortune was essential to my landing the prized telegram-boy job. The postmaster would phone my home to inform whoever answered (I wasn't allowed to answer the phone until I was about sixteen) that there was a telegram awaiting delivery. "Send the boy."

The payment was something like three pennies per mile, which was 'pennies from heaven', or a fortune at that time. Of course, shrewd businessman that the postmaster was, he deducted the cost of his phone call from my payment each time. I squirreled away those meager payments never spending any of it, and month-by-month it accumulated. The money was great but so too was the prestige. I got an arm band that said 'Telegram Boy' and a special belt with a small, leather, water-proof pouch in which I could carry the sealed message.

In summer it was a breeze doing these deliveries, perhaps just eight or ten per month. Even in the rain it wasn't much of a difficulty. Sometimes the addresses were just a mile or so away, but occasionally the trip was to the furthermost location seven miles up on the moorland.

Winter made the deliveries more challenging. One memorable, or should I say utterly unforgettable, trip was to a three or four house hamlet on the moors called Craigenputtock. It had been the home of Thomas Carlyle, a reclusive, but famous, Scottish writer in the eighteenth century. He succinctly summed up the isolation and bleakness of the place in a phrase, "Only he who wishes solitude would tarry here."

Carlyle's journeys to and from that place were completed in the relative comfort of a horse and buggy. I'd have added a more expletive-adorned description of my trip, by bicycle, in the unrelenting gale-force harshness of that winter night.

My Elswick had only one gear and the road was narrow, twisting and nearly all up hill. As it gets pitch black by 4:00 pm in December in Scotland, my bike was equipped with a dynamo for lighting. This mini generator created its meager glimmer proportionate to the speed of travel. The tiny, ribbed rotation-gear was held firmly against the bike tire with the consequence that the candlepower output was dependent on how fast I could pump the pedals.

I'd been strongly forewarned by the postmaster, "Deliver it whether there's anybody at home or not. Wedge it under the door or through the window if need be and tell a neighbour you've left it there." He obviously didn't want to pay for a second trip the next day. So deliver it I did.

The return trip, while nearly all down hill, traded speed for safety. Even at a suicidal rate, the headlight shone a mere fifteen feet ahead, which meant the frequent sharp corners of the road came up with horrifying suddenness. It must be mentioned that the frugal land-use planning of Scottish country roads left a minimal verge of grass before the impaling, jagged, whinstone walls that lined the roadways.

A further impediment in some sections was the dearth of fences or walls beyond gated sections that delineated the extent of each particular estate. Opening and closing the gates posed a further challenge as wheeling the bike through, and propping it up to allow closure of the gate, caused momentary, stygian blackness. I finally arrived home cold, wet, and weary, but very pleased with the tidy sum of pennies in my pocket.

(Those gates were, of course, there for a purpose, which became evident on future trips with fearful close encounters with the free ranging, five-foot-horn-span Highland cattle or herds of sheep.)

Over the miles and years I hoarded enough cash to buy a real bike when I was fifteen. I'd taken great care of the Elswick and benefitted, to my delight, from the new-fangled idea of 'trade-in value'. I got a substantial discount on the new model. It was a four-gear, drop-handle-bar, racing Rudge Pathfinder with toe clips on the pedals. It even had a retractable stand so I could set it up anywhere without having to prop it against the wall. Its dynamo could produce road illumination thirty feet ahead. I was in heaven, and the envy of the countryside.

By this time, I travelled twelve miles to the town school by double-decker bus. Arriving home about five pm on many a winter's night, a fast-growing, starving teenager ready to sit down to supper, I found that there were disadvantages to being the bike-rider in the family. My mother, bless her soul, smoked a packet of cigarettes each day and her addiction was the cause of frequent requests to bike up to the village store. My mood matched the local name for that hill, the 'Black Brae' on many of these swear-filled, rain soaked journeys but, as so often happens, unexpected good resulted. As I angrily forced each pedal stroke I told myself, "I'll never smoke!" and more than half a century later I still proudly abstain from that habit, remembering the vow I'd made on those excursions.

About that same time, my obsession with football enabled me to win a place in the village 'fitba' team. Once a week through the summer, on occasions when rain was uncharacteristically absent,

I'd decline the offer of a ride on the team bus and instead cycled the ten or twelve miles to neighbouring villages to take part in the game. It never occurred to me that I might be tired out before the match, but was gleeful that my return home was predictably ahead of the bus, which would have been significantly delayed by the need for a players' post game 'analysis' for an hour or so in the ever conveniently located pub.

Another memorable escapade on my bike was when a visiting family member left his spectacles at our home when he got on the bus to go ten miles to the train station in Dumfries. I'll concede that the double-decker bus made a circuitous journey around the country roads, but it was with immense pride that the Rudge Pathfinder lived up to its name, taking the shortest route and had me there ahead of the bus to hand over the errant eye-wear to a much surprised and relieved Uncle Bill.

As my world travels continued over the subsequent thirty years, the famous bike was carefully garaged at the old family home. I'd take the opportunity to do a few country rides on each annual visit home and was surprised at how I needed to select much lower gears than I could recall from days gone by, on hills that were also steeper. Reluctantly, heartrendingly, I finally took the faithful steed to a second-hand bike shop. With a tear in my eye, I asked the shopkeeper what he'd give me for the still magnificent machine. He wheeled it around for a bit, checked the brakes, dynamo and gearshift then spat out, "I'll gee ye twenty quid."

Reflexively I almost shouted, "What did you say?"

"Oh all right, thirty pounds tops," he conceded.

I tried to frown to cover my amazement. He'd just offered twice what the thirty year old bike had originally cost. I took the money but today I wish I'd kept the bike. With good care I'm sure it would still be roadworthy, at half a century vintage, with ten thousand miles and a million memories for the boy on the bike.

Be Prepared

On my honour I promise that I will do my best,
To do my duty to God and the King.
To help other people at all times,
And to obey the scout law.

*W*hen I was eleven years old, my family's encouragement to join the village troop of Boy Scouts was yet one more of the decisions they made that had a profound influence on my development. The 'Scouts' Promise' provided a guideline that engendered the ideals of good citizenship in me at an early age.

A new minister of the village church had announced that he was interested in starting a group, and a dozen or so young local lads joined right at ground level by cleaning out and painting a former stable and making it into our Scout Hut. That was the beginning of a camaraderie that would endure though rain or shine for years to come. We learned to tie knots; to bind and lash ropes; sing camp fire songs; practise Morse code and compass work; study astronomy; enjoy hiking and camping; and most importantly, develop self reliance, teamwork and bonding.

The lure of each of the distinctive little badges pushed us into efforts in areas which we'd have otherwise avoided as teenagers. Some of it wasn't exactly macho stuff but the 'crossed needles' badge proved we'd learned to sew on a button, patch a hole in a torn trouser knee or darn a sock, skills few of our male school friends could perform. The effort I put in at school to improve my study of French was spurred on by the desire to get the coveted 'interpreter's' badge. The 'first-aid' badge required knowledge of bandaging, splinting and pulse-taking and was, perhaps, a subliminal indicator pointing me toward my life-long career in medical matters.

The wholesome outdoor activity of hiking over the moorland to rendezvous with others on some bleak, windswept, rain-lashed crag, miles from the nearest shepherd's cottage, was part of the requirement to attain the 'pioneer' certificate. It bred in me the perseverance and stamina that has helped me through life. Of course it wasn't all fun at the time. Working against the clock to arrive at a map-coordinate miles the other side of a thigh-deep creek, or remaining undetected on a rain-soaked heather slope while other patrols searched the area was rigorous work. But often the hunt was more exciting than a Scottish Highland movie thriller.

I needed a kilt for my Scout's uniform and somehow my Nana found the money to buy a kilt for me when I was thirteen. At the time it fitted almost from armpit to ankle, but she assured me I'd grow into it. (She'd be thrilled that I can still wear it sixty years later, but it doesn't give great leeway for deep breathing nowadays.) For the uninitiated, let me inform you, a kilt, heavy when new, quadruples its weight after a few hours of being dragged through the bogs and wet hedges of southern Scotland.

Scouting was my ticket to travel and make friends. It took me to gatherings in the Highlands, camping in the English Lake District, and to competitions in Scout craft in other diverse locations. We raised funds for these distant excursions by performing 'bob-a-job' work parties, such as picking stones from farmers' fields. I achieved the Queen's Scout qualification after much study and two sleeves-full of badges, and was rewarded with a trip to Windsor Castle, near London in 1954. There, the new young monarch inspected our parade and passed no more than two feet in front of my smiling face. She didn't say, "Hullo Blair." Maybe she was just shy.

The crowning glory of my Scouting years was being chosen to attend the eighth World Jamboree at Niagara-On-the Lake, Ontario, Canada, when I was sixteen. Being one of eleven thousand Scouts from seventy-one countries was every Boy Scout's faint hope, our dream. That adventure gave my self-esteem a great boost and did much to banish the shyness and lack of confidence that had plagued me as a youngster.

Although not quite what Lord Baden Powell would have envisaged, that trip also gave me one unexpected but memorable human encounter. My dear old neighbour and friend, Mrs. Lawrie, hearing of my planned visit to Canada, asked me to visit her then eighty year old brother who had immigrated to Toronto in 1905. She hadn't seen him in fifty years.

Splendidly dressed in my kilt and multi-badged shirt, I took a bus to near the address she'd given me. It was in a rather run-down, older area of the city and I was obliged to ask for directions from two ladies on a street corner. The boy from the wee village in Scotland was a bit taken aback by their friendliness and laughter and was really quite surprised by the scantiness of their clothing. At first I thought they were perhaps trying to catch the sun's rays, and then it dawned on me what they did for a living. I scampered off with an instant crimson sun-tan of my own.

Returning from that four week trip, including a two week stay with a host family in Toronto, I was two days late for the start of my final year of school. The required visit to the office to find my designated classroom delayed my arrival to the first lesson by ten minutes. I opened the door to face a notorious tyrant of a teacher who didn't appreciate my tardiness and the interruption of his lesson.

"Who are you, and why are you late?" he bellowed.

Normally I would have cowered and nearly died but the new me answered, "I'm Blair Farish and I'm late because I was selected to attend a World Scout Jamboree in Canada." I even forgot to say "Sir."

"Why that's wonderful, Farish. I'd like you to tell the class about your travels sometime. Have a seat, please," he said, in an almost unrecognizably civil voice. I nearly collapsed into the vacant desk, suffering after-shock.

Scouting also gave me the opportunity to meet people that I'd never have encountered in the quiet working-class environment of the local village. One of the annual expeditions was a competition held on the estate of an aristocratic family who could trace their lineage back to the Jacobite rebellion in the 1700's.

The Scout Commissioner, the current Lord of the Manor, had done his bit for King and country behind enemy lines in Burma. He introduced elements of his commando background to toughen up the four-man patrols of young Scouts on weekend forays around his wooded country estate. We boys were thrilled by all the challenges. We had rope pulley-slides across rivers; went diving to retrieve pennies from a box in a deep pool; scrambled up and down former army assault nets; did rock climbing; and improvised a stretcher to carry one of our team members. It was all the stuff of dreams. My heart races at the memory.

I also had the good fortune to meet another member of society's upper class. From his majestic castle home, Walter Duncan, was a great benefactor who contributed immensely to Scouting in Dumfrieshire. He too hosted camp-competition weekends on his estate, but with less rugged expectations of dare-devil activities. He'd supply huge bins of food stuffs, with menus for all meals that each patrol had to cook on their own campfire. To make sure all the competing teams engaged fully we were asked to set out an extra place ready for a visitor, and unannounced, either he or his wife would be the surprise dinner guest. These were challenging situations, often accompanied by rain, and just to make things more interesting, nasty biting midges.

After supper the whole group was invited into our hosts' amazing home, up the spiral staircase to the one hundred-foot high tower, where his ancestors had defended themselves against rival clan invaders centuries earlier. We followed around through the huge library lined with thousands of books, passed Persian carpets on walls, and saw priceless masterpiece paintings and artefacts from foreign lands such as Ibex horns and elephants' hoofs made into foot stools.

That lovely elderly couple had a wonderful way of relaxing the visiting, boggle-eyed youngsters in that alien environment.

The Duncans had converted their ancestral home into a rehabilitation centre for wounded Norwegian servicemen during the war and we were fascinated with the countless photos and memorabilia of those days. Trinkets and photos of South Africa brought us back to Scouting, as our hosts reminded us how Baden Powell's original vision of the Boy Scout Organization was nurtured during skirmishes in the two hundred seventeen day siege of Mafeking in 1899.

On my return from Malaya, a decade later, I brought back a present for these two great hosts in gratitude for their kindness to me in earlier years. It was a preserved eight-inch wingspan butterfly that I felt would fit into their world wide collection of keepsakes. As Walter Duncan opened the box his eyes sparkled and he roared with delight. Of course I should have guessed he'd know something about it. His range of knowledge of the minutiae of worldly happenings, places, people and the obscure was legend. He sat me down for enlightenment.

"It's a Rajah Brooke. It's named after Captain Brooke who was the Queen's representative of the English Province in Borneo." He paused to let me gather that he meant Queen Victoria, and a nineteenth century event. "I was at Cambridge University with his grandson before the war. How kind of you to bring such an exquisite gift. I'll set it in a place of honour in my library." Nothing in all my Scouting, education, or travels could have readied me to, 'be prepared', for that pride-filled moment.

"Fitba"

"Some people believe football is a matter of life and death. I am very disappointed in that attitude. I can assure you it is much, much more than that."

Bill Shankley, English Soccer Manager

*T*he word 'football' has potential for ambiguity. Around much of the world the round-ball game called 'football' is the dominant sport. In North America, despite its multi-racial populace, the game known world-wide as 'football' is called 'soccer'. For the game they call 'football' they have perversely queered the pitch, changed the rules, increased each teams' numbers and squeezed the ball into a tortured oblong shape. It is a different entity entirely from the real game of football.

While possibly not yet taking over the title of 'Sport of Kings', football or fitba as we name it, is the sport of Scotland. Aficionados of golf or curling may dispute this viewpoint, but fitba is the game every kid in the land of the kilt is brought up on. They love, dream of, and rave about it. They cross Hadrian's Wall and the English Channel to stand and fight behind their fitba standard, The Lion Rampant Banner.

In days gone by, in the back streets, schoolyards, and country cow pastures of Scotland, fitba was one of the few affordable leisure pursuits for even the penniless of the population. For a few shillings, a leather fitba could be hacked to death by a dozen urchins for years before it finally succumbed.

And so, into this milieu was born a future star, near the village of Dunscore, population 250, in the heather covered hills of southern Scotland. Expense be damned, the boy was given a size three fitba as soon as he could waddle. In those days, there, the first great joyous cry from the proud family wasn't, "He's taken his first step!" It was, "He's kicked the fitba!" I'm sure nowadays, Facebook, Twitter, cell phones and other incomprehensible forms of communication relay to the extended family, and the entire world, every detail of that auspicious happening. It wasn't quite like that in the early 1940's, but I do still have a much dog-eared and thumb-marked, black and white early Kodak moment of yours truly kicking a fitba half my size. That was the first record of a future blue-shirted Scottish International Star. Dream on!

Hamden Park Stadium in Glasgow, with a capacity of eighty thousand raging fans, is that city's answer to Yankee Stadium. It is the location where Scotland defeats every other nation, at least once every century. My own private version of Hamden Park was the field in front of our kitchen window. It was the envy of most team managers with waterlogged pitches. Mine had a dependable drainage system due to its thirty degree slope.

By age six, I spent every ounce of energy and every minute of daylight kicking my fitba up that hill, again and again, hitting it 'on the volley' as it rolled back down almost as fast as the uphill launch. That was as close as fitba gets to using a tennis practice wall. Over the years, I imagine I kicked that ball there, a million times. Tiger Woods became quite good by hitting a golf ball that often, but of course, he was only hitting a tiny wee ball.

As soon as I was in my mid-teens, I vied with other youths for a place in the village 'men's' fitba team. During the once per week practice on the semi-flat field near school, we'd first have to chase off the cattle, which were responsible for keeping the grass short. Unfortunately they were also likely to have left distinct aromatic evidence of their passing, necessitating skills of sidestepping by the players.

After the hour or so of 'kick about', the old lads, ancient relics of twenty to thirty-five years of age, would retire to the pub to debate, consider and select the team for the upcoming match against a neighbouring village. As the sweat of our earlier efforts cooled, we young hopefuls would zigzag around the village War Memorial on our bikes. Impatiently, we'd await pub closing time at 9:30 pm when the joyful or heartbreaking news arrived.

The little green sheet showing placements and naming each player was thumb- tacked to the Garage notice board. It was a known fact that only two or three of the eleven positions would be allocated to the up and coming youngsters. The majority of the names on the list, predictably as if etched in stone, had paid their dues and pints as members of the selection committee. The lads in our little group would disperse, the pace of pedals indicating the jubilation or desolation of each cyclist.

Winning a place on the team opened the door to euphoria for the few days before each big game. Away games, as far as ten or fifteen miles to the next village, involved travel by bus. The rickety, wooden-seated, thirty year old, fifteen passenger vehicle was all we knew so it seemed just fine. It could be conveniently hosed down after our return trip providing the opportunity to remove residual sweat, beer bottles, and evidence of bovine excreta that had fallen off our leather-cleated boots.

Our team bus was a far cry from the air-conditioned or heated vehicles used by our hockey youth here today. In fairness, our old jalopy would soon have perished attempting the frequent Cranbrook to Manitoba mid-winter, twelve-hour expeditions of our Western Hockey League teams.

Back then, the two or three youths on the team were happy to endure the Spartan conditions as we waited an extra hour in the bus while our mature team-mates replayed the match, kick by kick, in the local pub. Occasionally we were pleasantly surprised at the brevity of these post game celebrations when dispute and altercation with the opposition caused havoc. The subsequent premature eviction of our bruised, bloody-nosed warriors got us on the road home uncharacteristically early.

The National First Division team scouts didn't deign to search for future stars in the village games, so my dream to move to the big leagues was put on hold until I made the move south. I joined the army and was posted to a Medical Corps training hospital in Woolwich, near London. Having had some difficulty achieving a permanent place in the village team, I should have had some insight into what lay ahead. There was a great unlikelihood of being quickly identified and selected from amongst London's ten million.

The naivety of youth is a blinding thing in the real world. The first hiccup occurred, and desolation set in, when I didn't merit a place in the hospital soccer team. I practiced with them and had the amazing learning experience that offered, playing amongst high skill-level members of the team.

In the late 1950's, military conscription dragged in, screaming as they came, all the young professional soccer players to do their National Service two-year mandatory stint. Managers and owners of the top league teams, horrified at the prospect of potential loss of their star protégés, were quick to use their contacts and special connections to have their prize players drafted into the Medical Corps. Further tweaking on the 'old boy net' would then have these players posted to the closest army hospital.

Of course, unit Commanding Officers were very happy to have such brilliant players as part of their unit teams in their mid-week games. These young men were generally given 'non-injurious' jobs in the sport stores and only put in an appearance at work Tuesday mornings, and disappeared after pay parade on Thursday morning. I always wondered why they bothered to collect their army pay of twenty-eight shillings a week, ($3.00 now), a pittance compared to the fifty to one hundred pounds they were paid for their ninety minute Saturday matches.

As National Service enlistment slowed, I finally cracked the roster, and had the delight of playing beside these experts. It came about when the Instructor of the Physiotherapy School, quite out of the blue, approached me with an offer that seemed to be the answer to my football dreams. He was a keen observer of the unit games and had his eye on me. He had previously been a Guard's Regiment officer during the war. His former Commanding Officer, a Colonel who he still kept in touch with, happened to be the President of a 4th Division professional soccer team, Hounslow Town, in South West London. Through this 'old boy' connection, I was invited to attend a Hounslow Town training session to see if I had the talent to make the team. I was cautioned that this was just a look-see visit.

I was in heaven! Oblivious of the torrential rain that drenched me, I rode my little Vespa scooter from Woolwich the twenty miles to the venue near London airport, surviving the ten thousand fuming cars, buses and lorries that threatened to crush me.

Finding the water-logged pitch, I stripped down to shirt, shorts and boots and introduced myself to the coach who didn't deign to acknowledge my presence at his side. A blind man would have seen the absence of welcome. I realized that although the Colonel had asked/told him to have a look at me, coach would make up his own mind.

While other players dribbled balls around lines of marker cones and practiced throw-ins and penalty kicks, I stood there bouncing up and down, wet and cold, trying to keep my circulation moving. Time dragged on. Coach stood there, silent, hands in pockets, dry as a bone in a huge oilskin coat that covered ears to ankles. A flat bonnet was pulled down to almost cover his eyes. The inevitable cigarette drooped from his lower lip. He was a picture of joy.

A heavy soaked leather soccer ball lay a few yards in front of him. Without even looking at me, he said, "Kick it." I recalled a million kicks up the brae at my own little 'Hamden Park'. Deep down, I knew I wasn't one of the super-skilled dribblers of the ball. My strength was the reward for all that diligent practice on a Scottish hillside.

I felt a surge of confidence. I took my run up, placed my left foot the required four inches from the side of the ball, balanced my body perfectly, swept my right foot back then through to strike beautifully, on impact cleaving the ball cleanly from its puddle to fly miles, it seemed, in a magnificent parabolic arc. My eyes never left the ball as it sailed forty, fifty, sixty yards down the field. Conditions being factored in, it was an amazing kick. In any other circumstances, I know the refrain would be, 'and the crowd roared'.

The rain continued to plummet and the silence grew. I had anticipated at least a "not bad", but nothing was forthcoming. Looking into his expressionless face as the smoke from his cigarette drifted up his nose, I hoped he'd choke. Eventually the mouth moved, cascading an inch of ash down his coat, "Go get it."

Only the faint-hope clause kept me from invoking expletives, but I bit my lip and like an obedient Border collie, went to fetch it. I was commanded to do another half dozen futile kick and retrieve efforts. Then, surprisingly, I got to run around and pass with some of the other players in the squelching mud. Coach never did condescend to speak my name through that utterly disheartening experience, and as the group dispersed, I dragged on my rain-soaked coat and long pants over shorts and shirt, there having been no offer of a change room facility. Mounted on my sturdy Vespa, I morosely retraced my circuitous route to Woolwich.

Eventually, dried out by eleven pm, I dragged my weary body up to the classroom to catch up on the study time I had missed. I was surprised when the Instructor sauntered in at that late hour. Sid, the name we called him behind his back, was full of good cheer, and asked me how I'd enjoyed my visit to Hounslow. It was difficult to conjure up much enthusiasm about the previous five hours, but he listened with genuine interest and compassion as I described what I felt was my one and only trial for the big leagues. I thanked Sid for his help in arranging for that opportunity, but had to admit it had not gone well.

"Don't worry", he consoled me. He pressed his index finger to the side of his nose in a conspiratorial fashion and gave an exaggerated wink. "I'll have another word with the Colonel." I was horrified and dubious, yet secretly pleased about the chance for another encounter with coach.

I was invited to practice the next Thursday. The weather was sunny and dry, the roads seemed less crowded and amazingly coach addressed me by name. "Hullo, Blair," he said. "Glad to see you again." Translation: He'd received a huge tongue- lashing by the Colonel.

Deserved or not, I played for the reserve team the following Saturday in a game against Welling Town, near Woolwich. The pitch had a significant down-hill slope from one end. Taking goal kicks up hill in the first half was a challenge, but I was thrilled to see how far my kicks went into the opposition half in the last forty-five minutes.

After the game, the coach approached, and even made eye contact with me and with brevity uttered, "See you Tuesday for practice."

Wow! And cloud nine was still to come. I followed my teammates into the dressing room. Before the match, we had set our shoes tidily in a row against a wall, quite apart from where our clothes hung. I was the new kid on the block so had just followed by example on this. There, in my shoe, like a neon light in a dark room, was a crisp Bank of England one-pound note. I was a professional soccer player! I cannot refrain from explaining the magnitude of this payment. At that time, my army pay was only twice that amount. My ninety minutes of joy and glory had fetched me half my week's pay.

Sid had watched the game at the Colonel's side. He was almost as excited as I was with my debut as a professional soccer player in front of three hundred spectators. I played another four games, for that astronomical fee each time, but I finally bowed out. I needed to concentrate on my studies and pursue my physiotherapy career, which brought me success and joy for the next fifty years.

Oh, but I remember it so well, my days as a fitba pro!

The Postman's Knock

*W*hen I was eighteen, I was the recipient of my first pink slip, the firing notice from a six-month temporary job as an estate farm worker. I had been grateful to the local squire for the work, filling in the time awaiting my imminent call-up to do my required two years National Service in the armed forces. I had gained valuable experience cleaning out pig houses, herding cattle, driving tractors, feeding sheep and attending threshing crews on neighbouring farms. I also apprenticed at potato picking, hay making, stacking sheaves of oats, shawing and lifting turnips and many more sweat-inducing or freezing pastimes. It had kept me fit, put money in my pocket and helped pass the time awaiting the inevitable time in uniform.

The dismissal letter/work reference, to use in future enquires for employment, was hardly something I'd brandish proudly at interviews. "He was a good laborer. Reason for firing: No longer needed." It was dated Term Day, 28th November, 1956. Historically that was the day when there was movement of farm personnel. Generally farm workers had cottages, tied to their particular job, available to them. There was the dairyman's cottage, plowman's cottage, tractor man's cottage and so on, so it was imperative that each firing coincided with a hiring, as the house exchanges were part of the contract.

Inquires and applications for work by young men in those days had a predictable first question, "Have you done your National Service?" Other than for temporary work, if the answer was no, the interview was instantly over. You could understand the perspective employer's viewpoint. The new employee might work for only a few weeks then get their military call-up. The sticky point was that exactly two years later that same employer was obliged, by law, to rehire that individual.

By good fortune and family connections (it was who you know, not what you know) I got an opportunity to start in the post office in Dumfries the week after Term Day. The job was described as 'just for the Christmas rush'. That suited me fine, as I was certain my call-up would be any day soon. I reported that first Monday of December at 6:00 am and was issued an armband to say I was a temporary postman. I was also provided with a pair of waterproof leggings, a poncho, hat and a bike. At 6:15 I was on my way, accompanied by a vintage postie affectionately called Auld Wullie by all his colleagues. He was awaiting his retirement at the end of that year and had enough accumulated holiday time to be spared the frantic season of parcels, Christmas cards and letters that doubled the normal load of deliveries. He had two days to teach me all I needed to know about being a rural postie.

I was at pains to know how to address Auld Wullie. In deference to his age I started with 'Mr. Brown'. Seeing me perhaps as a young upstart, he never invited me to use a less formal title with him.

His first instruction was a silent adjusting of the knot in my tie and fiddling with my shirt collar to get it to meet with his liking. It was my first ever experience with a detachable collar with a flat back stud and longer front stud to connect the shirt and the collar components together. The collar was stiff and was already biting into my neck, but it didn't seem like a good time to mention this. I learned from him that the collar was reversible and could be turned over to show the clean side. Collars always came in pairs; consequently Monday and Wednesday offered a new clean collar that was reversed on Tuesday and Thursday. Friday and Saturday required salvaging the least ingrained surfaces. The same shirt lasted all week. Not appealing today, but I was renting one room in a lodging house in Dumfries that did not include a washing machine or dryer, so the shirt system worked well for me then.

The bike I'd been allocated was a heavy, antique, cumbersome model with a classic flat carrier shelf in front. Auld Wullie went over its attributes in detail and forewarned me that I'd have to carry a pump, puncture-mending kit, and tools to change the accompanying spare inner tube. I had a momentary sigh as I compared this one-gear carthorse of a bike to my sleek, drop-handle, racing model at home.

As the new kid I got the huge mailbag and load of parcels that had been presorted into bundles. "Tomorrow you'll be in at 5:30 am to do your own sorting," Auld Wullie advised me as we set off to travel north out of town. I wobbled along in his wake for a couple of miles of city streets till, on entering into the open country, I was invited to ride up beside him. For the next few hours over hill and dale he never stopped talking. There seemed to be a million things to tell me about the business of delivering letters to eighty houses over twenty-two miles.

At first I wasn't listening very carefully but then he said, "I'll be expecting you to tell me all this tomorrow you know." He got my attention there and then.

For the first hour or so, few houses were lit up, so he quietly slipped the letters through the mail slots in the doors, being careful to gently lower the lid silently. He'd give me a stage whisper biography of the residents, and all family members, what jobs they did, which son was courting the neighbour's daughter. It was a detailed commentary.

Auld Wullie's pace was unbelievably slow. In the first hour I could see that it was going to take us a full five hours to do the distance that I'd whiz round in an hour on my own bike. As we began to meet actual live bodies at the doors I began to understand that social interaction was part of the job. His discrete rap on the doorknocker was the signal to embark on protracted dialogue.

"How's your boy doing up in Glasgow, and, the lad over in Germany, and how's Jenny managing at her new job? Henry will be starting to swot up for his highers at the Academy now." This was all at one door where the sleepy-eyed mother of the clan tugged her dressing gown up tight to ward off the morning chill, but she was proud of Wullie's intimate knowledge of her family.

We arrived back at the post office five hours later. I was mentally exhausted by the oversaturation of information. Auld Wullie led me to a cramped cubicle at the back of the post office where we spent a fifteen minute break. As he indulged in his flask of tea and sandwiches he said, "You'll have to remember to bring a snack tomorrow." There was no indication that this was time off so in my nervousness I never thought to ask if I might nip out to a café to get a bite to eat.

For the two-hour afternoon shift we went to the railway station where Auld Wullie instructed me on the art of dragging huge mailbags off the trains onto trolleys. The trolleys conveyed the mailbags to different storage sheds where vans waited to take the mailbags to the post office. He sat on one of the big wheelbarrows and peppered me with details on how the job should be done. I worked up quite a sweat, and somewhat diffidently, asked him how on earth he managed to do all of this heavy physical work. He said, "Oh, I don't do any lifting at my age, you know. I get one or two of the young porters to do it for me, but I'm sure they won't do it for you."

When the work was done we hung around for quite a while, presumably to let me cool off, and finally made our way back to the main office. He cautioned me, perhaps pre-answering my unasked question about the delay. "Oh never get back too early. They'll just find you another job."

Two days with Auld Wullie was my full instruction time. I'd decided that the work was pretty straight-forward and in fact, easy. I was about to become a postman on my own. It didn't take long before I wished I'd paid more careful attention to his words of wisdom. My first day solo was a whole new learning experience, and a disaster.

My outward self-confidence was immediately suspect because I'd made sure I arrived fifteen minutes early for my 5:30 am start time. The old hands picked up on this and launched into a tirade of catcalls. These changed to derision as I began my sorting process. "One hour to sort twenty letters! That's about one every three minutes!" I was the brunt of everyone's humour that morning so by the time I finally had all my bundles of two hundred letters wrapped and wedged into the delivery bag, I was relieved, if not happy, to escape into the torrential rain.

The weather had been cold and windy, but dry, on the two days spent as Auld Wullie's apprentice, depriving me of instruction on how to keep myself and the mail dry in a downpour. The waterproof leggings were cumbersome, a bit like horse-riding chaps, and instantly hooked on the saddle as I first mounted the bike causing a near calamitous dismount. As I wobbled away, the poncho cape, designed to fit over my upper body, handle bars and the mailbag, blew up into my face in the first fifty yards, deluging me with a puddle that had already accumulated in its folds. I got off to reassemble the supposedly protective gear, glancing suspiciously to see if any of my fellow workers had witnessed the debacle. My few moments on foot reassembling my raingear had allowed the bicycle seat to become fully drenched which I only realized with horror when I was once again astride the saddle. It was an ominous start to my new career, soaked to the skin, (especially on parts of my body where the sun never shines) and still not a single letter delivered.

That first day solo continued to be a nightmare. Twice I needed to backtrack half a mile or so when a letter surfaced that I'd miss-sorted into the wrong bundle. Few were the cheerful smiles I'd received at Auld Wullie's side when I now apologetically handed over a rain soaked precious letter. (I learned that fountain pen ink blots quickly when wet.)

The two mile long, arrow-straight Holywood stretch, every inch of it directly into what had become a howling gale from the north, was the ultimate test of my endurance. Having to half-stand on the pedal on each down stroke, I berated the thoughtlessness of the Roman Legions who had created that particular shortest distance from A to B two thousand years earlier. Despite my previous silent prognostication that the entire delivery could be covered in two hours, that morning's six, rain-soaked hours holds in my memory as the longest day in history. As in so many learning experiences and trials in life, the laughing came later.

After what must rank as the shortest probationary two weeks, I was fitted out with a full post office worker uniform. My outfit was made of royal blue, heavy, worsted-serge material built for durability rather than comfort. The slacks and tunic jacket were warm in winter, sweat-inducing in summer and weighed twice as much when wet. Almost predictably, my first appearance as a full-fledged postie brought forth my fellow workers derision again: "Watch you don't cut yourself on those trouser creases," and much worse.

Out in the country the remarks were much kinder, even flattering, "Oh you do look smart now," I heard, as though I'd been a real scruff dressed in my own trousers and jacket in the first two weeks.

"Oh, you're a real man now," seemed open to ambiguity.

As Christmas approached the load of letters, Christmas cards and parcels became a challenge to sort out, wedge, and balance on the front metal carrier of the bike. But I gradually became familiar with the names in each house and farm, and found ways to deliver, relatively undamaged, all the mail on my route.

In the 1950's Christmas Day was not a holiday. The Queen's mail was still delivered to every household in Scotland. I'd heard chat in the sorting office about the tips that were anticipated, as Christmas perks, by many of the delivery staff but wasn't sure what might happen for a new postie. To my delight and surprise I was the recipient of all sorts of tokens of appreciation. The treasure accumulated house by house. A sixpence here, three pence there, a whole shilling, a box of shortbread, a dozen eggs, homemade sausage, four lamb chops and, unimaginably, from one of the great ancestral homes, delivered somewhat reluctantly by the butler, a crisp new Scottish pound note. It came with the caveat: "His Lordship assumes that you will share this with the normal postman."

"Oh but of course," I responded, trying to fathom out just how abnormal I was viewed by that gentleman. While monetary gifts were the norm, there were also offers of a wee dram from several households. I declined, to the surprise of these generous folks. (My upbringing in a staunch temperance household hadn't yet been destroyed by my subsequent nine years of the relative drunken debauchery of army barracks life.) During the return journey to the post office I perplexed over the need for fairness in dividing up the swag.

There was a distinctive celebrative atmosphere in the office. Some of the returning deliverymen had obviously not declined the offers of alcohol and a van had even been dispatched to try to locate one postie whose return was overdue by two hours. Auld Wullie, whose pre-retirement time off had suddenly run its full course, had popped back in just to say 'Happy Christmas' to all his old pals. It was a bit revealing that he just happened to be perched on the shelf of my sorting cubicle.

He had a mild air of bonhomie but wore a businesslike, firm set to his jaw. "And how are you managing the route?" he inquired solicitously. Without waiting for an answer he launched into his real reason for the visit. He had thought out his strategy and delivered his pitch without delay. "I've always found the folk on the route most generous at Christmas. The big house especially is reliably good for a pound. Now then, you realize that I did the job for eleven months and you've just been on it for a month." He let the silence do its work as sexagenarian eyeballed teenager. I tried a token attempt at negotiation but Auld Wullie had already done the arithmetic. I reluctantly handed over the lion's share of the swag including all the perishable goods that didn't appeal to me. The learning continued. On reflection later, I realized that it had been an entirely just division of the spoils.

Back on the route I gradually got to know the diverse personalities of that rural population. I learned to roll with the punches and to absorb gratefully the wonderful insights offered. I also learned to adapt the rigidity of the rules to the needs and the wishes of the people. Many were the occasions when caring outweighed the letter of the law, and each of those experiences helped make me the person I am today.

I fondly remember old Peter. A retired shepherd, a widower, he lived an isolated and lonely life in his little two-room cottage. It was perched on the brow of a hill, three fields from the nearest roadway. He still hiked down to the village shop two miles away, his rolling gait belying his seventy-five years. On his twice-weekly jaunts I'd occasionally overtake him on my bike and stop to pass the time of day. "I don't suppose you've any letters for me?" he'd ask.

"Not today, Peter," I almost invariably had to answer. Sadly, I can't recall ever delivering a hand-written letter to him in the six months I travelled that route.

That wasn't the real story of my connection with Peter, however, or how I came to know so much about him. Peter was an addict when it came to betting on the football scores. 'The pools' were something like the lotteries today. Littlewoods and Vernons Pools were a betting system for forecasting the results of the regular Saturday football matches. Little green envelopes came out every two weeks and, as a mixed blessing, I had the questionable pleasure of delivering these to many houses on my route, including to Peter's remote cottage. I couldn't leave the mailbag on the road so had to push the bike and load up through the three fields to his door, rain or shine. Every second Wednesday, Peter would be sitting, the kettle boiling, awaiting my arrival. "You'll just have a wee cup of tea with me," he'd say. I hadn't the heart to decline his offer because the habit had formed over the years that the postie would deliver that week's betting form and wait while Peter filled in his predictions of wins, losses and draws.

To compound this dereliction of duty, he'd delay me further by asking for my opinion. "Now then, how do you think Rangers will do against Celtic?" I'd sup my scalding tea giving him my opinion on the game he'd mentioned, always worrying that I was woefully uninformed in these matters. That wasn't a problem. He'd already decided long before my arrival, but it was part of the ritual between us. Glancing anxiously at my watch, I'd try to hurry him along.

Eventually it would all be done. He'd predict twenty-six games, calculate how much he'd bet, and tally up the amount. "So that will be two shillings and two pence and the stamp will be three pence, the postal order three pence." He'd pause before adding the crowning confirmation of illegality, "That will leave four pence for your bother." That was my pay for purchasing the illicit cheque and stamp in town, and mailing the whole lot that afternoon so that it would be valid, postmarked long before the matches were played.

I'd finish my cup of tea, pocket the shillings and betting form, and make my way back through the fields to the road. Although this activity was clearly beyond the duties of the postie, and furthermore occasionally was used as convenient cause for dismissal of non-performing posties, the powers that be generally turned a blind eye on those common 'irregularities'.

The visit to the 'Big Hoose' on my route was an eye-opener for me. Pedaling my bike through the massive iron gateway at the lodge and up the winding driveway sheltered by the centuries-old great oaks and rhododendron bushes, it was hard not to feel intimidated by the grandiose ancestral home. I'd park my bike in the side archway at the servants' door, take off my poncho and leggings, and hang them where the beaters left their raincoats on pheasant shooting days.

Up the back staircase and into the kitchen I'd haul my mailbag and sit at my assigned corner table. The mansion had been the family home for seven generations and the incumbent Lord, Sir Francis*, had been knighted for his deeds of daring in some far-off outpost of the Empire. (Despite his efforts in the Khyber Pass, British troops continue to fight the same futile war today but no longer wear the easily-targeted scarlet tunics and pith helmets.)

Sir Francis* had financial interests all over the world and had fascinating mail from exotic locations. The postage stamps themselves told the stories of tea plantations in Assam, diamond fields in Africa, cattle in Australia and furs from the distant Hudson Bay Company. Additionally, the mail to that household had an extra nuisance factor. Each day, wrapped in brown labels, newspapers arrived to keep the great man up-to-date on the business world. The Times of London, Manchester Guardian, The Daily Telegraph, The Glasgow Herald, and occasionally, overseas airmailed editions of The New York Times, Chicago Tribune and the Wall Street Journal all were delivered by the postie.

Larger in size than the average letter, these rolled up newspapers were prone to more dampness than the other mail. The butler would go into a tizzy if I was late or the newspapers were wet. He'd whip out the iron and do his best to flatten and dry each paper before laying them in pre-determined order on the tray, beside the coffee carafe and cup and saucer, that he then conveyed into the inner sanctums, presumably Sir Francis'* study or bedroom.

Tradition, generosity and kindness of that great family ordained that the postie would be given a full Scottish breakfast every day. It included sausage, eggs, beans, fried tomatoes and mushrooms, toast, tea, and even H.P. Sauce.

I vividly recall my first meeting with Sir Francis*. I was wedged into the little corner table, a sort of out-of-the-way location where the kitchen staff tolerated my presence. The heat of the kitchen caused my soaked trouser legs to steam. Disheveled and mid-egg, my appearance was in glaring contrast to the great man's elegance as he sauntered into the kitchen.

He was majestic from top to toe. His silver mop of wavy hair and bronzed complexion, evidence of a recent excursion to some sun-drenched far off place, contrasted sharply with my dreary, white pallor from the sun-starved Scottish winter. Even his maroon dressing gown with its gold trim and matching tassel-ended sash had the appearance of made-to-measure for his impressive physique. The sealskin slippers, that today would provoke the ire of the animal rights aficionados, made me squirm realizing my shoes still held some evidence of recent steps into unmentionable animal excreta in the farm courtyards.

He casually surveyed the scene. The butler, in a bit of a flap finalizing the morning tray with tardy mail and newspapers, apologized profusely for the delay. Sir Francis* sized up the situation, came over and addressed me with friendly forgiveness and kindness and said, "Shocking day out there, Postie. Glad you made it through the storm."

I was in great turmoil. I didn't know whether to try to stand up and speak with my mouth full, or just to sit and splutter and choke. I blushed and nodded. He laid a gentle reassuring hand on my shoulder to console me. He said good morning to the maid and assured the butler, "No rush, there Williams," then made his exit as smoothly as a cruise liner leaving port.

Some days later I saw him in his Rolls Royce. The driver gave me the 'no-see' glare but Sir Francis* was kind enough to give a smile and a pseudo-regal wave of recognition. I tipped my hat in response, almost falling off my bike in the endeavor.

From time to time I'd see him at a distance, tromping the fields, shot gun at hand, conversing with the game keeper, no doubt assessing the pheasant and grouse population in readiness for one of the estate's upcoming shoots. Once too, crossing a bridge at the edge of the property, the same gamekeeper gave me an exaggerated, pantomimed hush command to ensure that I didn't disturb the Lord salmon fishing nearby.

A few years later, I'd be using this very infrequent connection with the aristocracy to do some advantageous name-dropping in a far-off place where I had finally achieved a similarly bronzed visage. That would be delayed pay-off from my days as a rural postie.

Grave Undertakings

*M*y family's involvement in the business of death and burial dates back to 1818 when an enterprising father and son hung up their shingle announcing they were in the undertaking business. At that time it was quite logical that the village carpenters, or joiners as they were described in Scotland, would be the tradesmen who could make coffins. Down through the generations, sons and nephews followed in their forebear's footsteps carrying on the traditional ways of that long established company.

My Uncle Dick, the last in the family business, persevered years after he had retired from the carpentry side of work to reluctantly act as funeral director for some local families in their time of need.

"Ye buried ma faither, his faither and ma great-grand faither before him, so ye canna refuse the family now!"

Finally, in his mid eighties, the sprightly old veteran plucked up enough courage to decline further entreaties for his services, making one of his classic humorous statements, "I won't wear this suit again till it's needed for my own funeral."

The outfit he was referring to was the traditional jet-black dress suit of officialdom. It had fit him better when he had returned from the war in 1946 as a slim young man in his early thirties. Discrete expansion gussets had since been added to the back of the trouser waist band to accommodate his increasing girth over the decades. The ensemble was a source of great entertainment as family members laboured to wedge him into what had once been the essence of sartorial elegance. Watching him ease carefully into the front seat of the hearse en route to the graveyard, we would take bets on the probability that his almost-throttling starched shirt collar would pop its front and back fastening studs before his return.

It was a family tradition, as long as I can remember, that we would gather round the kitchen table the evening after each burial to hear about the solemn occasion. The normalcy of this was never questioned, even though it was often the mishaps and humorous events of the day that were described.

"Aye, Jimmy the older son, dropped his cord so the faither went doon heid first," Dick would say, straight faced. (In those days six family members would each hold a rope, or cord, to lower the coffin into the eight foot depth of the grave.) "And then Uncle Tam's top hat fell in after it. We had an awful time rescuing that bonnet."

The hilarity of these funeral evenings was not disrespectful. On the contrary, it was our way of honouring and saying good-bye by acknowledging the naturalness, including all the funny parts, of the ritual of death. My old friend and mentor, Jimmy the miller, swaying on his way home past our house following his evening pint or two at the pub, once dallied momentarily to catch the gist of the loud laughter coming from Broombush. A day or two later he casually mentioned, "Ye were havin' a fine old time the other night. I suppose ye were celebrating Jock's funeral."

Nothing got the old family home rocking better than the tales of unforgettable mishaps in the undertaking business. Even as late as the 1950's, coffins were built in the carpenter's workshop. Subsequently, the finished polished-mahogany work of art was transported to the home of the deceased. There, the body would be laid gently in the coffin's satin-lined interior to lie in state till the day of burial. We could imagine my uncle's embarrassment when he told us of once arriving at a distant shepherd's cottage to perform this solemn practice in front of the assembled family, only to find that his utility trailer was devoid of the new coffin. It was pitch black as he retraced his path, searching for the casket that had strayed from its bonds. "Oh I had a good idea of where it would be," he said, and true enough, five miles back, the wooden chest lay undamaged at the side of the creek whose hump-back road bridge had caused its escape.

Some of the old country homes had not been designed to facilitate the removal of coffins through the front door. This was especially so where add-on porches had been built as fashion trends, and the need for heat-conservation dictated building changes. Before the advent of funeral homes, Uncle Dick had many tales of getting an occupied casket out through the cottage window.

A favourite story described a new young minister's trials and tribulations on a particularly wet and blustery day. It was early on in the days when cremation was almost an unmentionable word. Surprisingly, old Henry had opted for this new-fangled method, and had asked that his ashes be spread amongst the beautiful flowers that he had nurtured and doted over in his small garden.

Twenty-three year old Reverend Wilson*, with his brand spanking new starched white collar digging into his Adams Apple, was obviously ill at ease as he cowered beneath the umbrella that was fighting a losing battle with the elements. To his horror, he observed little rivulets of rain creep across the leather cover of his very recent gift of a King James Bible. It had been his graduation present from his proud parents, who had had it embossed with almost obscenely large gold lettering, John Arthur Paul Wilson. To speed things up he selected a short reading from a page whose wrinkle and watermarks would in future always remind him of that day.

Henry's ashes, in a screw top glass jar, were grossly uncooperative as the preacher intoned, "Ashes to ashes, dust to dust," and threw open the jar with a wide sweep of his arm. Most of the jar's contents, immediately soaked, settled onto the drenched ministerial gown and the clothing of the assembled mourners. It was hard to say whether the flowers benefited from the nutrient potential of the few specks of ash that made it into the garden.

I must clarify that these 'celebrations' of ours were never liquor enhanced. For generations the Farish family had been rigorous teetotallers, intolerant of any suspicion of alcohol, and encouraged by the almost tyrannical 'Wee Free Church' dictums against booze.

Others in the surrounding communities were not affected by similar restrictions and another book or so could be written about the goings-on at wakes which the Scots and Irish seem to have perfected. Years later, I felt obligated to counter this omission in my early education, and must concede that, as in all controlled use of pseudo-medicinal potions, there are potential benefits in the soothing use of such beverages, although my memory is sketchy about those trial lessons.

The undertaking business had its challenges, and we had many anecdotes relating to the serious part of the profession. We knew about sorrow and bereavement, and no-one was more caring and supportive than my family members in time of need. The humorous stories, though, took away much of the fear and superstition associated with that most inevitable fact of nature, death. Stories of how a limb had to be, "…bent a wee bit or wedged to fit," brought howls of cathartic laughter and, I believe, gave me a healthy outlook on the reality of death. It was an education that helped me to cope more easily than many of my peers at times of death in hospital wards, and even in my occasional work in morgues during my military career overseas.

That background may even have been a factor in my current volunteer involvement as a member of the Fort Steele Cemetery Society. This group oversees the restoration and ongoing planning of that beautiful historical burial site. Close to the original North West Mounted Police barracks of the late 1800's, the graveyard lists names of pioneers of yesteryear and is a popular final resting place for local residents.

It is comfort to me that I have my own plot reserved in that tranquil location, nestled near the magnificence of the Rocky Mountain peaks where I've climbed and scrambled. I like to hope that, with luck, my ongoing interest in the burials there might stretch out to 2018, marking two hundred years since my family first started helping with funeral arrangements, back in Scotland.

I encourage everyone to do their part in lessening the anguish of the time of their death by having, at least, made plans for the physical disposal of their remains. Perhaps my wee limerick might open up the opportunity to make this often taboo subject into a family-friendly discussion matter rather than a grave undertaking.

Gone So Soon

An old man on his way to the grave,
Did his best to stay calm and be brave.
He'd no fears or obsessions,
How they'd split his possessions,
That he'd worked all his life just to save.

For one fact that gave him a thrill
A job done just before he fell ill,
He discussed with a friend
Well before his sad end,
And had written a most detailed will.

And the facts that he wrote on the sheet,
Were in order and tidy and neat,
Such as who, when and where,
What kind of coffin to bear,
Whether ashes or still legs and feet.

And his wealth he'd divide on that page,
No child should be rich at young age,
And the minutest things,
Such as dogs, cats, and rings,
Planned with foresight as best he could gauge.

On his epitaph words clear that say
Do it now, do it soon, don't delay
Be prepared – look ahead,
It's too late, when you're dead,
The time for your will is today.

Depot Daze

*T*he late night train from Scotland taking me south to my army career didn't exactly offer first class accommodation for the new recruit. I found myself wedged into a six-seat compartment with seven other young men and their luggage. Most of them were in uniform, returning from forty-eight-hour leave passes in Glasgow, and had already adopted the military strategy, "If you're not working, sleep."

I'd foolishly chosen to wear the new blazer that my family had bought for me when I left high school. It had the school crest, with Minerva, goddess of wisdom, fluttering her wings on the pocket. D.A.F.P.A (Dumfries Academy Former Pupils Association) initials brought me great pride, but by the time the train reached Annan, fifteen miles into the journey, it had become the topic of ridicule and hilarity. "Hey, Dafpa," in an intoxicated Glasgow dialect wears thin quickly.

At Crewe, at 3 am, there was a mass exodus to the all-night cafe during the train's ten minute stopover. The old hands at this game had bolted before the train came to a halt. As the newest, least experienced, I was at the end of the line-up for a sausage roll and mug of tea. More troops had poured onto the train so by the time I returned to take my seat it was occupied by a huge, belligerent, inebriated paratrooper. I explained to him that he'd taken my seat. His unprintable response challenged me to do something about it, so I prudently joined the dozen or so extra bodies standing in the corridor for the remainder of the four hours to London. There I figured out the tube train connection to Waterloo Station where it seemed the entire British Army was assembled waiting for departures for Aldershot and all-points military in the south of England.

During the two hour wait at Waterloo Station I learned another new skill. Many of the uniformed lads quickly bought a Daily Express newspaper, spread it out carefully on the concrete station platform, adopted the horizontal position, and instantly fell asleep. I envied them, but although tired after my sleepless ten-hour journey, I couldn't risk missing my train, or messing up my much maligned blazer.

"All passengers board the train at number three platform for Woking, Farnborough, Fleet, Basingstoke, Winchester and Southampton." There was a mad surge of Army, Air Force and Navy uniforms, and an assortment of us bewildered recruits in civilian dress. We scrambled aboard and the train clattered across the switches on the multiple diversions in southwest London's rail system. There was a mass exodus of 'the Brylcreem Boys', as the Air Force members were called, at Farnborough. The next stop at Fleet was my destination as it was the nearest station for Aldershot and Crookam, the Royal Army Medical Corps depot.

The Navy gang en route for ports on the English Channel spread out in comfort in the vacated seats, as I staggered off the train holding my one little suitcase. We were little huddles of lost souls standing around waiting when a khaki-uniformed fellow with one chevron on his sleeve approached and took command. "All right, you lot, R.A.M.C. recruits, over 'ere". He was a cockney and cocky with it. He ushered us toward a truck and bullied us aboard. To the uninitiated, he was king, and only later we discovered he'd been in the army only three months.

The fifteen minute journey to Crookham, all of us standing, swaying about in the back of that vehicle, was not conducive to conversation. We stumbled out grasping our meagre belongings. His shouted orders had us scurrying across the parking lot as soon as our feet hit the tarmac. We half ran to an isolated one-storey building where another twenty bleary-eyed, frightened young men waited. We melded with them, all equally unsure of our future.

A figure strutted forward, stopped in front of the assembled group and let a purposeful silence hang, for what seemed ages, to get our attention. He had two stripes on his arm, so was presumably twice as malicious as our first tyrant, who had returned to the truck. Our new boss introduced himself in a surprisingly quiet voice. "I'm Corporal Jones*. You'll address me as Corporal Jones. Who am I?"

There was a disjointed mumbling from the group, "You're Corporal Jones." He went into a tirade about not being able to hear us and again demanded "Who am I?" in decibels that must have carried for miles. It took five tries before he was satisfied with our response. He then herded us like reluctant sheep to the barracks. Ordered inside, we each stopped by the nearest bed space, dumped our bags on the bed, and assembled facing the central corridor. That was too easy. Of course we couldn't stay where we had randomly ended up. We were reshuffled to our places in strict alphabetical order. After a lot of staggering and shoving, we stowed our worldly goods in the six-foot tall army lockers and awaited the next item on the agenda.

"Right, you scruffy lot, form a line and leave by that door. As you exit the building, grab a mug, knife, fork and spoon. There will be no replacements, so guard those items with your life." We gathered outside and were ordered to get into three ranks which, since we didn't know what that meant, took a lot of shouting and shuffling to achieve. "Hold your K.F.S. and mug in your left hand, behind your back. By the left, quick march, 'eft oight'eft oight 'eft oight," shouted Corporal Jones.

In the cook-house we joined a long line inching its way toward the serving area. We each picked up a plate and approached an assembly line of cooks guarding individual cauldrons of sausage, mashed potatoes, steaming cabbage and gravy. Looking ahead we could see that the process involved presenting our plate below the front edge of the huge canisters so that the cook could serve that item by slopping the contents of their ladle of food onto the waiting plate. The technique required striking the shaft of the serving spoon on the metal rim of the container thus dislodging the quota onto the plate. The finesse of this manoeuvre required accurate placement of the plate three inches below the rim of the container. Inevitably, about every twentieth nervous new recruit would misjudge that critical height. The ladle would then smash the plate to the accompanying shout from the cook, "Back of the line," informing the poor lad to get a new plate and join the queue behind the next hundred or so in line. The choices in the menu were take it or leave it. We each gobbled down the unappetising fare and ten minutes later were back outside.

We stumbled the three hundred yards back to our barrack room, deposited K.F.S. and mugs in our lockers, marched past the cookhouse to the distant clothing stores. In single line we approached the counter top where the storesman spread out a poncho/groundsheet/cape. He glanced at the recruit in front of him and in a practiced second determined height and weight and demanded, "shoe size". Then, fast as an auctioneer he shouted out names of items as he threw them from the shelves: Shirts, three; underpants, three; undervests, three; trousers two; and so it went for it seemed another one hundred items. We tried to contain the mass of equipment in the poncho as we more or less marched back to the barrack room, dropping items every so often. As the last recruit dumped his load of kit on his bed, Corporal Jones* appeared, in his new personae as 'Mr. Tidy'.

We watched in awe as he attacked one of the heaps of clothes and equipment and had them neatly folded and stacked in the locker in ninety seconds. He stood back to let us see the exactitude and precision of placement of each item. Of course, so that there was no favouritism shown to that lucky fellow whose kit was tidied away, it took a further ten seconds to scatter the locker's entire contents across the room.

"I'll be back in twenty minutes and every item will be in place as shown." Right on schedule, he was back as we tried to stuff the final unwieldy great coats and webbing straps into the bulging shelves.

"Right, get those civilian clothes into a suitcase or bag. They are going home." He produced cardboard mailing labels and string. "Say goodbye to all that crap. You're in the army now." I anguished over my blazer as I carefully folded it into my small suitcase. Minerva's wings were no longer white, but splattered with cabbage-green and my gray slacks had gravy on them.

We struggled into itchy, hairy shirts, stockings, ill-fitting trousers and boots that felt like steel rather than leather. He had given us half an hour to ourselves and the room took on an angry buzz as we lost our individual identities in the sea of khaki uniforms. When he returned the order, "By your beds," it got us rigidly into our allotted spaces with our lockers open. He found fault in every one, and jettisoned items with a flick of his drill stick. It was clearly a well-practiced art because be could send the displeasing article half the length of the room.

It was 4:30..oops, 16:30 hours. (We'd been warned never to use civilian time measurement.) "Fall in outside for supper parade." Of course we now knew that meant K.F.S. and mug in left hand. The lunch time line-up debacle was repeated. On the return march to the barrack room, the "eft oight eft oight" pace had speeded up, as if there was great urgency to get to the destination. Entering the room the first few inside flopped spread-eagle onto their beds. The penance for that indiscretion was a full, non-stop five minute "Attenshun, stand-at-ease" repetition for the entire household.

It seemed like the day would never end. Two 'volunteers' were ordered to bring in two boxes of supplies that they distributed: Candle, one; box of fifty matches, one; soup spoon, one; cherry blossom boot polish, black, tins one; 12'x12' cotton rag, one....

Corporal Jones* then explained that we'd light the candle using only one match, heat up the spoon and press it onto the thousand little bumps on the two pairs of leather boots that we each had issued to us. "I'll expect the toe caps to be smooth and the first five layers of polish applied before lights out," we were warned. Over the next four hours there were thirty different #!&!#^ describing the stupidity, absurdity and futility of this task.

Punctual to the second, he returned to announce, "Lights out in thirty seconds." He did two lengths of the room flicking socks, boots, and belts onto the floor waving his badge of authority, his drill stick. At the doorway he flicked the switches off bringing pitch darkness to the place. "Reveille, 05:30," was his last utterance before we heard the door closing to his own private room, just down the corridor.

There was a gradual build up of frantic searching, muttering and cursing as we tried to locate lost equipment and get our bedding untangled from the heap it was still in. The first few candles sputtered into pinpoint light sources.

With a crash that stopped every heartbeat in the place, Corporal Jones* was back. By the time he turned on the light switches the half dozen lit candles had been extinguished, but the tell tale smoke lingered in the air. He charged down the three-foot space between the rows of beds. "Everybody, down, twenty push-ups." When nobody owned up to lighting the candles it was, "Down another twenty push ups." Few of us could comply, which didn't please him, but with a final order, "Total silence," he stormed off making sure the room was again in blackness. That had seemed like the longest day of my life, and the night wasn't any better. I endured the two-inch thick mattress on the wire spring bed, but the alien sounds of snoring, farting, and noisy dreamers made for a general feeling of unease and restlessness. I got very little sleep.

Day two didn't start well either as we were double marched to the cookhouse five minutes after reveille at 05:30. The porridge and milk proved challenging when I realised I'd lost my spoon and nobody lent me theirs. Right after lunch we were marched to a new set of huts where single lines of men were already formed at the doors. We duly took our place and entered three or four at a time where an eighteen year old (undoubtedly former carpenter's apprentice) cut our hair to fit the army slogan "What's inside the hat is yours, every other visible inch of scalp belongs to the army and will be hairless." Most of us had had the foresight to get a brutally short civilian haircut in anticipation of our upcoming enlistment. Nevertheless, in the era of the 'ducktail' and a full Elvis-like mop, it was a forlorn, silent, shorn bunch that lined up to march back to our barrack.

Boot camp was scheduled to last twelve weeks. Interspersed with hours of marching, or square bashing, as it was called, our education continued with such fundamentals as how to iron razor sharp creases on our trousers; to cover belts and webbing straps with protective messy layers of blanco paste; to polish belt buckles, uniform buttons and badges with 'Brasso'; and shrink the issued army beret till it fitted like a skull cap, except for the overhang on the right which had to be one inch above the ear.

Gradually we learned some of the fundamentals of medical knowledge and practice that would make us competent 'medics', able to offer the expertise that would save lives on the battle field. By the time six weeks had passed we'd learned a lot. We could run carrying a 'volunteer' on a stretcher; apply a Thomas splint on a fractured hip; and revive a patient using artificial respiration, as CPR was then called. We practiced injecting syringes of murky water into oranges which were supposed to imitate the texture of human skin. To achieve the 'real thing' atmosphere, we drew straws to see who would lay in the bottom of a muddy trench as a mock patient, while the rest of us applied shell dressings and bandages.

Although there was unrelenting pressure to perform from dawn to dusk most of us learned to roll with the punches throughout it all. We dropped three or four from our original thirty, most because of their inability to keep up with the physical demands of the regime. We were kept sane with the natural evolving of humour and leg-pulling and the start of camaraderie that created lifelong friendships. So too, our tolerance of the squad instructor improved as we figured out which minor infractions were most likely to send him berserk.

As we got into more serious lectures on military matters and first aid, he'd pause to ascertain whether we had understood the material presented. He'd look up and quite civilly ask if we had any questions. Once only, our regular squad comedian stuck up his hand to indicate he had a question. Quite pleasantly, the Corporal said, "Yes, you in the back row, what's your question."

Straight faced, the lad said, "I just wondered, Corporal, can we smoke?" There was total silence as we all held our breath knowing the answer would be painful.

"You'll bloody well smoke alright, Laddie. Everybody down, twenty push ups, one, two, three..." It's really quite difficult to do push-ups while you are laughing silently.

We had two or three squad comics whose pranks kept the overall spirit of our group balanced and more able to tolerate the absurdity of some of the things we were asked to do. Our marching and precision drill had advanced unrecognisably as we about turned, double marched, saluted and a dozen other mundane manoeuvres. The squad instructors, bored no doubt with the repetitiveness of drill square activities, would spice things up occasionally by playing a sort of chicken game. They'd march us head on towards an oncoming squad, hold the collision course to screech the about turn command at the last second. At times like those, someone in the squad invariably tried to get us to stretch out our pace to make the catastrophe happen.

Crookham was less than ten miles from Farnborough, home of the Royal Air Force. In the 1950's it was a common occurrence to have the gargantuan Vulcan Delta Wing Bombers complete take-off right over our depot drill square. The marching squad could hear the ominous noise of the jet engines as they started on their two mile take-off, and the plane's hundred-foot wing span cast a shadow over the puny squads below. Sometimes the deafening noise would almost drown out the drill instructor's commands and the agitators would whisper, "Disregard, disregard," in the hope of making the squad march into the embankment at the edge of the square. Of course it would have brought about the death sentence if it had ever happened.

As we advanced through training we'd get Saturday and Sunday afternoons with no scheduled training. Mischief set in on one of those occasions when one of our group initiated a mock full-squad march to the main-gate guard room. There our clown asked for permission to march his squad out the gates across the road to the entrepreneurial tattoo parlour conveniently situated there. Bored and accepting the harmlessness of the prank, the request was granted. The entertainment of the mission faded for me as I realised the expected compliance of each of us. Despite much harassment from our peers, only six of us declined to get the obligatory tatoo. During the following week, the festering new images rubbed painfully on the scratchy shirt material, but the discomfort only brought more scorn directed at the 'wimps' who had been too chicken to become 'real soldiers'.

Despite all the apparently pointless and degrading elements of army basic training, compounded on occasion by stupid pranks and inconsiderate interpersonal attitudes in the group of recruits, life went on and camaraderie soothed wounds. Much whining occurred amongst the troops with the sentiment of the day usually being, "I hate the x!#?en army." I'm sure that was a common feeling in military locations all over Britain. I'm well aware that R.A.M.C. training was a 'walk in the park' compared to the rigors faced by young lads in the regiments.

An interesting post script occurred a quarter of a century later which reinforced the notion that memory of life's black moments often fades over time. The 1982 announcement of going to war to retake the postage-stamp sized South Atlantic outpost and historical British Dependency, the Falkland Islands brought about a stampede to reenlist. Former, "I hate the army," National Servicemen of the 1950's were desperate to get back into uniform with belated patriotic zeal. Their rejection saved them from that seventy-four day war. The suffering, and the two hundred fifty-seven British military deaths, is documented in books such as Simon Weston's, *Walking Tall*.

During my seventh week at Crookham I was ordered to present myself before an older, placid Captain. Alarmed that I might be 'back squaded', a process of retaking parts of the training for failure to achieve, I was very nervous. He had a file with my name clearly on its cover. "What's this about you wanting to be a physiotherapist?" he asked in a gentle voice. "Do sit down and relax I won't bite you."

I was a bit taken aback, as this was not in line with what I'd become enured to, an environment where everybody shouted commands and questions. Carefully I lowered myself onto the chair, doing my best to sit at what would be 'attention'. I struggled to explain how I liked the idea of that branch of medical training, trying to pop in a comment or two about aspects of the work that Sgt. McGregor* had stumbled over in my first recruitment enquiry.

The T.T.O. or Technical Training Officer explained that it was his job to look more thoroughly into applications such as mine. "You've got the education requirements," he said, reviewing my chart, "but the problem is you've only done seven weeks basic training and the new school year up in Woolwich is starting in ten days time. You're supposed to do twelve weeks here at the depot and must complete the final "pass class" exam."

I hadn't an answer for that situation. He browsed through my documents for a few more minutes. "I'll tell you what we can do," he said. "There's one of these final exams being held in two days time. I'll give you a chit to excuse you from all the training, marching and that sort of rubbish. You hit the books every hour of the day, pass that exam and I'll get you on that course."

Fate had intervened and I was certainly going to do my best to take advantage of the opportunity. I crammed from dawn to midnight, passed the test and was given permission to begin the physiotherapy course at Woolwich. I even had time for five days leave that I spent in Scotland.

Corporal Jones had the last word of course, peeved that I'd skipped out almost four weeks early. "With only seven weeks of training, you'll never be a real soldier," were his farewell words. I was oblivious. I had survived the bewildering stress of the Depot Daze. I was on the way to my chosen career.

The Royal Herbert Hospital

I was intimidated and in awe as I stood in front of the great archway entrance of the Royal Herbert Hospital, in Woolwich just outside London. The Herbert was the military training centre for nurses, x-ray and laboratory technicians, and physiotherapists.

The first foundation stone for the hospital had been laid in 1861. Built in the then new pavilion-style, the twenty-five wards were three stories high, along the main long corridor. Accommodating six hundred-fifty patient beds, one for every ten military personnel in the immense Woolwich Garrison at the time, it was palatial by the standards of the day.

The spacious, high-ceilinged, well-vented wards owed their existence in part to the zealous campaign for health reforms by Florence Nightingale. She had recently returned from the Crimean War where she'd been sent as an observer by war secretary, Sidney Herbert. There 'the lady with the lamp' and a courageous group of nurses had pioneered progressive changes in medical care requiring hygiene and fresh air as vital components in healing the sick. When Queen Victoria commanded that a new hospital be built to replace the century old Garrison hospital, Captain Douglas Galton (later Sir) of the Royal Engineers was appointed as the architect. He just happened to be Florence Nightingale's nephew, so it's no great surprise that her opinions would be implemented in the £209,000 structure. (It is of note that today, each of the two hundred twenty-eight luxurious, privately-owned apartments created in the original building, and named the Royal Herbert Pavilions, cost in excess of that sum.) In 1900, Her Majesty Queen Victoria visited the Herbert Hospital and was so impressed that she granted it Royal Patronage, thus the Royal Herbert was born.

I stood there, equally impressed, until a voice called, "Hey you, move yourself. Who are you?" The Corporal in charge of the sentry door at the side pedestrian walkway stood menacingly tall. I explained that I had come to be enrolled in the physiotherapy school. "Oh, you're one of them, are you? How long have you been in the R.A.M.C.?"

"Seven weeks," I hesitantly whispered, not daring to make it eight if I counted the week of leave I'd just finished.

He roared with laughter. "You're still a sprog," he said, using jargon for the newest of new recruits. "Well, we'll let you take off those depot squad flashes now that you're in a real army unit." I'd forgotten to remove the tell-tale black shoulder markers and blushed at my oversight. He came to my rescue by asking, "Do you play football?" The magic words thrilled me, and started a great friendship between us. I found out that he was a National Serviceman who had landed a cushy job where he could get liberal time off to play professionally for Portsmouth Town in the English First Division league.

He directed me to the Administration Office where they did the required paper work and asked me the usual fifty questions. When one of the not-so-usual questions was, "Do you play football?" I knew I was in the right place. I was made to feel even more welcome when the young clerk did a ceremonial scissor removal of my offending and embarrassing depot insignia.

I hauled my kit to Barrack Room Eight to meet my ten new family members, the living-in component of the first year class of the school of physiotherapy. Our new home on the second floor had large, vertical-sliding windows with the old sash-cord mechanism. The windows opened onto the seemingly constant roar of traffic on the four-lane Shooters' Hill Road. I immediately noticed a two-bed rather cramped alcove that faced away from the road and onto the peacefulness of the hospital gardens and tennis court. A young fellow Scot had already monopolised one of the beds there so I quickly took possession of the neighbouring bed and locker, glad to meet a countryman. He'd been in the army almost a year and had already had significant nursing experience. His cheery disposition soon got us settled into a comfortable friendship.

The day went by and the other beds got their residents as the full quota of the new class arrived from various hospitals around the UK. We were a mixed bunch - some National Servicemen in for their two years, one infantryman who had re-enlisted and chosen to try the Medical Corps, and a former medical school student who had dropped out of university after three years. We had multinational representation as well: One Irishman, two Scots, one Welshman and six Englishmen, all with incomprehensible dialects. A 'Geordie"' from Newcastle, a 'Scouser' (Liverpudlian) who probably went to the same school as one of the Beatles, two Cockneys from home-town London, a guitar-playing quiet lad from Devon, and a Yorkshireman. Capping it off, there was our Middle Eastern representative, Corporal Mohammed Ali bin Yousef, a delightful Jordanian who could hardly speak a word of any of our languages.

As we all sorted out our kit and bunched up together for supper in the cookhouse we gradually got onto first name terms, or at least the names we gave each other, quite inoffensively. The two Scots of course were labelled Big Jock and Little Jock, the Irishman was Paddy, the Welshman, Taffy, and our friendly Arab was abbreviated to Ali. That sorted out, the free evening drew some of us to the Navy, Army, Air Force Institute (called Naafi) Canteen, while a small group chose to check out the neighbourhood pub.

Anticipating an important first visit to the school classrooms next morning, most of us got settled into bed fairly early. The guitar man played softly for a while and all was well. Eventually the four pub crawlers made their boisterous return. There was a bit of disgruntled exchange for a while but gradually things settled down peacefully.

It seemed just minutes later, but was really six solid hours, when the night duty Corporal stormed through the building announcing reveille. I could hear his approach five rooms away, and still attuned to the recent depot regime, I was up and dressed before he banged open our room door with, "Feet on the floor, wakey, wakey, it's 06:30." I was boggled-eyed observing a few of my new roommates slowly struggle to the sitting position whilst other's turned over and pulled their blankets more snugly round their necks. Expecting all hell to let loose at this blatant defiance, I was shocked to hear the Corporal's only protest being an even louder slamming of the door as he left. This was a different army. Gradually most of us got shaved and showered, ambled down for breakfast, tidied up our bed spaces and set off for the 07:45 roll call parade. The last of our tribe rushed down at the last second, still knotting ties and buttoning tunics as they answered their names.

Straight after parade we made our way to the school to start our new careers as physiotherapy trainees. In the classroom we met one more R.A.M.C. lad who lived in married quarters, and four female nursing corps students. The Staff Sergeant instructor had already decided where we'd each be seated and gave us the briefest of welcomes before getting down to real business.

"Right, row one, you'll collect dusters and dust all desks, clean blackboards, tidy and dust the bones in that glass case and wash the sinks." Each row of us was allocated cleaning jobs and duties. "These tasks will occupy you from 08:00 to 09:00 Monday to Friday. On Saturdays 08:00 till noon you'll clean the physiotherapy department and clinical training rooms and gym. There'll be no swapping the jobs you've been given. Any questions? Right, get to it."

We learned his name was Sid from members of the senior class. He had been a war-time Guards' Officer who had re-enlisted and qualified as a physiotherapy instructor. He was still a Guardsman at heart despite the R.A.M.C. initials on his sleeve. There was a groundswell of muttered discontent as we set about our chores. This reached a crescendo when we got out of sight on our mid-morning twenty-minute Naafi break. It didn't soothe our angst to hear that the senior class got that first hour for study period each day, excused from manual labour.

At 09:00 the school principal, chief lecturer, and undisputed boss entered the classroom. He was short, bald, dressed in a tweed jacket with leather elbow patches and had a deceptive smile. A retired former Sergeant Major with twenty-five years of service, he now lived in the Officers' Mess as a civilian, and thrived on that status. We leapt to attention as he came in. "Please be seated ladies and gentlemen," he said. "I'm Arthur Smith, your Principal. You can address me as Mr. Smith or Sir. In future you needn't stand when I enter."

The smile vanished as he got down to business. "Let me see, ah yes," he scanned the room for affect. "So there are sixteen of you. Let's get something straight, right now. I expect hard work from each of you. You'll have a three-hour written exam every three weeks. Failing marks will not be tolerated." He let that information sink in, but there was worse news ahead. "There will be only ten of you remaining at the end of your first year. Of these, perhaps four will be invited to continue to become civilian qualified physiotherapists. Do I make myself clear? Any questions?"

Hearing none, his smile returned, he swivelled and left, marching into the next room to start a lecture to the senior class. In the silence that followed, I kept thinking, "But Sergeant McGregor*, you promised me my chosen career!" The prospect of a seventy-five percent mortality rate sucked the very soul from each of us. That feeling wasn't improved when we learned that the five in the senior class had started out as fifteen.

Then next hour saw us each issued with note books, massive texts on electrotherapy, physiotherapy, exercise therapy, and the bible of everything about the human body, the 1597 page *Gray's Anatomy 29*[th] *Edition* updated considerably since its first printing in 1858. We started right in with four hours of lectures that afternoon. Exhausted we staggered down for supper at five o'clock to return half an hour later for the first of the compulsory ninety-minute evening study sessions that would be our daily lot Monday to Thursday for the next year.

Despite his austere countenance, 'Arthur' as we daren't call him, was a brilliant teacher. He knew his stuff. His speciality was anatomy. He'd build amazing drawings on the blackboard starting with the bones. Every tubercle, sulcus, eminence, groove, and condyle appeared picture-perfect from the great book. Each ligament seemed to be glued onto its attachment, then tendons stretched through the appropriate tunnels, nerves and blood vessels intertwined and stimulated and fed their corresponding tissues.

Every lecture was enthralling. It was a million years before photocopying, overhead projectors and Google, so we handwrote and tried to copy his intricate diagrams into our notebooks. He'd leave the drawings on the board overnight and I'm sure he knew that we checked every tiny detail against the original renditions in *Gray's,* hoping for an error (not that we'd ever dare to bring it to his attention). Not once in that whole year did we find a glitch. The other two instructors were equally diligent in presenting exercise physiotherapy, theory and practice of electrical treatments, massage, gym classes, pathology of disease, and orthopaedics. It went on, seemingly nonstop dawn to dusk including the dreaded evening study, but I found the content fascinating.

The third Friday crept up on us with the three-hour written exam as promised. It was a silent, solemn group that handed in their best efforts at the punctual 'pens down' order. Arthur took the papers home. That evening, as we checked anxiously for the answers in the text books, discussing amongst ourselves our best guesses and getting into a dither about our questionable longevity in the school, the stress level was palpable. Eventually, the boozers hit the pubs and the non-drinkers were sorely tempted to join them.

Next day we mumbled through the morning four hour cleaning chores but then all worry was forgotten. Several of us boarded bus, train and underground tube to arrive at my first ever First Division football match. Watching Arsenal play at Chelsea was the ultimate antidote to the ravages of the preceding weeks. I'd never been squashed into a crowd of forty-seven thousand before. It was unimaginable for the wee boy from the village of Dunscore. What a thrill! Now that was fitba.

After a supper of fish and chips wrapped in newspaper, we moved on to another first for me, a West End theatre show. Our surrounding audience members in the cheap 'nose bleed' seats inches below the ceiling, a long distance from the stage, were less than pleased with the vinegar and salt residual aroma of the army lot, and did some pathetic mumbling and complaining. It didn't lessen my enjoyment of the evening one bit. Both that afternoon and evening were a therapeutic release from our pent up tensions. We caroused our way back to the Herbert, sober yet intoxicated by the delights of the day.

The blood pressure was back to critical level on Monday morning. It was clear the boss hadn't had nearly as good time as we'd had over the weekend. You could have heard a pin drop after he slapped the papers onto the lectern in front of the class. He let us all fester for what seemed an hour, but was really only twenty seconds of absolute silence. His smile vanished. Then he started briskly. "Wilson, 88%," pause, "quite encouraging. Evans, 83% - sound effort; Pearson, 78% - good; Brown ,75%. You are a former medical student; I am very disappointed with your mark." On it went. We sweated it out. Despondency set in as lower marks followed. "Farish, 57% - you'll have to pull up your socks." I darn near died. Down and down went the marks. "Corporal Mohammed, your grasp of English is not up to snuff, so I haven't given you a number." In the pause we heard Ali asked his desk partner, "What mean snuff?" Nobody laughed.

Little Jock's name came up at last. "I won't humiliate you in front of your peers by mentioning a number. You have a cheerful disposition. You'll make an excellent nursing orderly. Pack up your books."

Wee Jock showed us all what he was made of. He stood, picked up his books, and said in a strong, purposefully-accented voice, "Thank you, Sirr. It's been fun," and marched out the door, head held high. He was posted to another hospital next day, and from the grapevine we learned he excelled in nursing through his remaining years of service.

Meanwhile, back in the 'salt mines', the evening compulsory ninety minutes of study stretched voluntarily to three or four hours for some of us. My marks crept up ever so slowly and I hit seventy percent just before Christmas. We lost one class member each exam till then. Before Easter one girl quit, and one got married which forced her departure from the army. At the final exam in July, I awaited the final decision-making very anxiously. We were taken into the office individually and told our fate. As Arthur Smith had predicted, only ten of us had survived the culling during that year. The three National Servicemen had only one year or less to serve and none of them were interested in signing on for longer terms, so were posted to UK army hospitals as physiotherapy assistants. Of the seven remaining, only four would be invited to continue on in the school. I made the cut. I was 'one of the few', or the four to be exact. I felt like sending a post card to my recruiting maestro, Sgt. MᶜGregor*.

Of course, there was a price. The army wasn't going to train us for three and a half years unless we committed to a full nine-year service engagement. I was overjoyed with the invitation to stay, and I loved what I'd learned so far and couldn't imagine leaving it to try some other pursuit. Although I'd worked extremely hard, there had also been some great times in sports, socialising, seeing London, and learning just how wonderful the camaraderie could be in military life. It didn't take a nano-second to answer the boss's question about signing on 'for nine'. He shook my hand and seemed sincere and pleased to welcome me to the senior class for my next two years in the school's program. "I knew you could do it," he said. "Welcome to the team."

The following two years also provided diverse exposure in other locations. We were farmed out, at the Army's expense, for all sorts of short-term visits to specialized therapeutic centres in London's famous hospitals and rehab environments, and even some further afield. Short duration 'experience' postings to other army hospitals around the country brought variety and fun, but it was always pleasing to return to Woolwich which had become home to me.

As our studies continued we got individual tuition to help us pass the progressive levels of the National Civilian Exams each year. With the three-week exam pressures removed, things got a bit more forgiving, and the Boss smiled more often. And always in the background, caring in his own unique and often impatient ways was Staff Sergeant 'Sid', the assistant instructor and disciplinarian. He was also the one who gave me my memorable, short-lived flirt with professional soccer. Rugby, cricket, tennis, entertainment, and the wee Vespa balanced out study to make for an enjoyable, and relatively normal, life. Two new chevrons on the arm also helped me cope with some of the 'idiot-synchronies' of army life.

A joyous reunion of six of the original physio-school chums occurred at a friend's fiftieth wedding anniversary in 2009, in Vancouver. That reconnection added to the regular email communication we 'Herberts' maintained. Sadly two of the close gang from our original school class had passed on, so the memories of that great era become more precious each day. None of us will ever forget our amazing good fortune of being trained at the Royal Herbert Hospital.

The Wee Vespa

*I*t is hard to conjure up a list of good things that arise from the ashes of war, but the Vespa motor scooter is one of the fortunate outcomes of turmoil in Europe. Part of the agreement for post war industry restrictions was the cessation of production in the once renowned fighter aircraft factories near Milan in Northern Italy. This coincided with the need for inexpensive motorised transport for the population at that time. There had been earlier prototypes of that kind of vehicle manufactured in America as light, versatile machines to be used by their armed forces. Paratroopers launched themselves and their scooters from planes, and found the instantly accessible, rugged, motorized bikes ideal for the rough country and pot-holed roads of war torn Europe. Ironically these originals were the modes of transport used in the retaking of Axis-controlled Italy. These machines got the name of Paparino (Donald Duck) for their ugly shape. The new challenge was to produce a peacetime, inexpensive, easy to ride vehicle that could carry two passengers. It was also expected to protect riders from the elements and dirt.

In 1946 the Vespa was born. It originated from the matching up of empty mechanical shops and warehouses, with a skilled workforce of aircraft engineers and designers suddenly redundant from their professions. These former aircraft builders combined precision and aerodynamic design to come up with the required specifications. The result was a new industry that would produce fifteen million of the popular scooters over the next half century.

The name, Vespa, meaning wasp, came about from two of its distinct features. It had a thick body section housing the engine and rear wheel, connected by a narrow waist to the wing-like front wheel and steering canopy. Early models also had a bit of a whiney 'zing' sound produced by the tiny two-stroke engine. With a svelte, eye-catching body design and bright colours, the Vespa hit Europe. Over the years, it appeared from Salerno to Singapore, Saigon to Saskatchewan. By 1956 one million had been sold, no doubt aided by the vision of a Vespa-riding Gregory Peck and his gorgeous pillion passenger, Audrey Hepburn, in the 1952 popular movie 'Roman Holiday'.

The summer of 1958 found me a survivor of my challenging first year in the Army School of Physiotherapy. Our original sixteen student compliment had suffered severe astringent attrition to ten. Only four of us accepted the invitation to continue for the balance of the three-year program which would gain us graduation as full-fledged civilian-qualified physiotherapists. The move to second year meant that I'd remain in the UK and in the environment of the army school and teaching hospitals.

I had devoted so much time to studies and sports that I realised there was something missing in my life. I was by nature very shy and easily embarrassed and especially uncomfortable in my dealings with the opposite sex. I didn't drink alcohol and so avoided the much bragged about cavorting in the pubs and dance halls near the hospital. I needed some 'magic potion' to overcome my frailties.

My pals tried to inveigle me into the smoke-filled caverns of the Saturday all-nighter clubs but the noise didn't appeal to me. I fled from one such 'den of iniquity' on overhearing a scantily dressed, heavily painted, inebriated young lady describing me to her friends. "He doesn't drink, he doesn't smoke or anything." It was the, "or anything" that galvanised my hasty retreat.

Days later it dawned on me that what I needed was a smoke, drug and noise-free environment, with pleasant female companionship, preferably in the country far from the congestion of London. The magic item that could offer these pre-requisites was a Vespa scooter. It was the ultimate 'chick magnet'.

I travelled by bus the three miles to Welling the next Saturday afternoon. I negotiated feebly because I was already smitten, and contracted to buy a 125cc beauty for the unimaginable price of one hundred twenty-five pounds sterling. The cost was almost a whole year's army pay, but with some savings, and a substantial pay-later high-interest loan, I could do it. It took a whole week of cajoling, lying and pledging my future earnings to make the deal happen, but on the following Saturday I became the inordinately proud owner of my first Vespa.

In the 50's, my car driving licence and a large L-plate gave me full sanction to hit the highway on two wheels. Money in hand, the salesman spent a cursory three minutes to fully instruct me on all I needed to know: "Fuel on, reserve, off switch; clutch; handle bar gearshift lever; mirror; parking stand lever; lights; brakes; accelerator; kick start," he intoned. A quick drag on his cigarette, then he continued briefly, "Carburetor; choke; left and right indicators; foot brake." Seven further seconds covered balance and things to avoid like pedestrians, other traffic and stray dogs. He sauntered off. It was the easiest sale he'd ever made.

I sat on the seat, feet touching the ground for balance, instantly envisioning the first pretty pillion passenger who'd be entranced by the magic of it all. Obviously, for safety, she'd cling to my welcoming torso, snug behind her 'knight in armour', on such a magnificent steed.

Wobbling a few circuits round that tiny lot, it dawned on me that facing the raging traffic was preferable to damaging the many other bikes parked there awaiting new owners. First gear was just fine for the next two hundred yards. Even at maximum engine revs it only produced a manageable ten miles per hour, as I meandered and wobbled along using the full width of my lane. Honking drivers crowded up behind me, less pleased with my snail's pace.

Eventually I prodded the complaining clutch/gear-shift mechanism to engage second gear. The poor engine almost stalled, then struggled bravely back up to its forward propulsion revs. Sweating profusely, I looked ahead to the ominous traffic lights which had turned red leaving me with less than fifty yards to halt my now enthusiastic bike. I managed to brake just in time.

From there I lulled myself into an almost comfortable state on the long gentle slope up Shooter's Hill Road. I was still in second gear but my self confidence was slowly returning when tragedy struck. The engine sputtered and stalled and, due to my unpractised use of the clutch to deal with the loss of power, I was unsaddled, in slow motion, onto the grass by the roadside. A few honks and derisive shouts from the passing vehicles left deep scars in my psyche.

Once I had levered the bike upright and got it parked on its stand, a slow circuit of inspection brought massive relief. There was not a scratch on the paint work. I'd spent a futile five minutes trying to coax the engine into life, when a fellow biker stopped to offer his help. He rode an older Lambretta scooter, the rival make, obviously at least six months vintage, but 'any port in a storm'.

He asked me what had happened. He glimpsed at the speedometer which, like a beacon, showed only 1.1 miles driven and tried hard to suppress his laughter. His diagnosis, then treatment, took all of five seconds. He pointed to the petrol control lever which was set at OFF. "There's usually about a mile's worth of fuel in the pipe after you turn it off," he said. Belatedly, I recalled my instructor/salesman demonstrating the workings of said switch. The rescue angel turned the switch, pressed once on the kick starter and my machine purred like a kitten. There was a hint of flamboyance as he mounted his bike, had it into third gear in thirty yards, and swung nonchalantly into the traffic even daring to give a long lasting wave of farewell.

My confidence and pride in tatters, I didn't dare make a stop at the top of the hill to drink in the view, but managed to slowly cruise the long downhill stretch to the hospital with its magnificent Victorian Archway. I succeeded in manoeuvring through my 'Arc de Triomphe', even negotiating the cobblestone courtyard with a glimmer of panache. Safely parked at the edge of one of the paved pathways, I removed a few particles of dust from the windshield using a clean handkerchief and, as if by magic, I had an audience of three rather cute nurses.

"Wow! What a beautiful bike," one said, oozing charm. "How long have you had it?" cooed another with a brilliant smile. I puffed up my chest and stood every inch of my six foot height, and with a confidence I'd never before experienced, laughed and said, "Twenty-nine minutes." The third nurse cut in with, "Will you take me for a ride on it someday?" I darn near swooned. The 'chick magnet' was in top gear.

As an L-class driver, the next month dragged on endlessly. L-plates dictated that I couldn't take on a passenger until I'd passed my test. I'd become a reasonably accomplished driver by then and had put on nearly a thousand miles. The great day arrived when an unsuspecting young beauty agreed to travel out into the countryside as my passenger.

It was a time when nobody wore crash helmets and my ardour-induced blindness let me overlook the need for warm jackets. The sun was shining and I kept the speed at a gentle thirty mph. I was on cloud nine and didn't notice the building up of actual rain clouds. Not ten miles into our journey the heavens opened up. The deluge only lasted a few minutes but we were in the middle of a five-mile open stretch of road without a glimpse of shelter.

We turned around and made our non-communicative return to base. Her previously warm arms that had snugly encircled my waist, as I'd advised to ensure her balance and safety, suddenly found a preferable secure grip on the chrome pannier frame at the back of the seat. My heartfelt apologies didn't merit a response from her at the front of the hospital where she insisted on dismounting rather than be seen with me. Her shiny new shoes were sodden as she squelched through the puddles. Her gorgeous long, blonde hair was now bedraggled, and her beautiful pink dress, drenched.

I realised that courting a fair young maid wasn't as straight forward as I'd hoped, even with that 'ace up my sleeve', a brand new Vespa. Subsequently, there seemed to be a dearth of volunteers for my pillion seat. No doubt, "That son of a bitch tried to drown me!" got around the hospital like wildfire. So, for a while, I kept a low profile on the amorous front. There were to be many memorable adventures, and inevitably misadventures too with the Vespa, but none as depressingly calamitous as that first venture into the not so 'bright blue yonder'.

The wee bike became a reliable, convenient source of transportation that opened up many new exciting pursuits. I became a frequent visitor, albeit spectator, at Brands Hatch automobile and motor cycle racing circuit just twenty miles south of London. At the time, it was a kidney-shaped circuit of 1.1 miles, and thus it offered spectacular viewing of the entire track. This provided close-up observation of the immense speed on the straightaways and yet allowed sufficient proximity to the hairpin bends to see the skulduggery and tactics that are part of high- speed racing.

Today's map of the extended 2.3 mile circuit brings back wonderful memories of yesteryear's world leaders. Brabham Straight, Graham Hill Bend, Surtee's Corner and Stirling Moss Bend all are sign posts of glorious days of the past. Others who raced there include Steve McQueen, the movie star, and a good friend and fellow burn survivor, Peter Procter who had converted from world class bicycle racing to become a brightly decorated winner in sports car racing.

An added thrill to finish off an already exciting day at the races at Brands Hatch involved leaving the race course half-way through the last event to rush a few miles up the main highway towards London. On a mile-long straight section cut thought the rolling hillside, the steep embankment on each side was a prime viewing location to observe the post race madness. Sometimes these grassy banks were crammed with spectators.

A distant roar from the south signalled the mass start of the street bikes, high powered monsters that could reach a hundred miles per hour or 'break the ton', as it was then described. Six abreast at times, close-knitted bunches of thirty or forty of them would scream past, their pillion seat passengers clinging on tenaciously, flirting with death. At the end of the mad stampede of hot-shots, groups of those hillside spectators, adrenalin goaded, would create a slower yet scary follow-up of the earlier maniacs. Amongst the last to leave, my 125 cc 'put-put' was enough for me at its maximum fifty-three mph.

In addition to pleasure rides, sightseeing and exploring, the Vespa was also a utility vehicle for my frequent inter-hospital moves. I had acceded to pressure from the school principal to wear a helmet. To face the fairly likely rain and cold of some of my journeys, a gift from a former war-time air crew member was a great addition to my wardrobe. It was a full, 'ears-to-ankle' flying suit and was part of the many stories of memorable near-miss survival incidents of its former aviator, and its new two-wheeled speedster owner.

One such close call occurred as I travelled from Chester where I'd been sent for specialized training under the direction of the Army Physical Training Corps remedial gymnasts. I'd been granted a week's leave and sped towards Scotland. My route took me up over a bleak, windy and rain drenched summit pass named Shap Fell.

The bike was grossly overloaded with a huge suitcase wedged across the well space, behind the shelter of the front canopy, where my legs should have been tucked. This meant my knees poked out each side into the near blizzard as I crouched behind the high windshield. Behind the seat on the chrome luggage rack, I'd secured a large wooden, former ammunition box, sturdy of make but weighing a ton, filled with the rest of my worldly possessions.

Balance, manoeuvrability and safety were grossly compromised, and the heavy load did nothing for top speed capability. To add to the discomfort, the driving position created a pouch-like dip in the front of the flying suit and the knees winged-out position channelled the torrential rain to that spot. It didn't take a genius to figure out that the heavy brass zippers were not waterproof. Therefore, the next four hours were filled with extreme discomfort, especially in private areas of my body.

To distract me from such matters, I followed a grimy smoke-belching truck for a mile or so of the climb, both truck and Vespa grossly overloaded, and each labouring in second and first gear. Near the top the hill the road flattened out a bit so, having endured as much pollution as I could tolerate, I edged my quarter-ton load past the forty-ton behemoth. I couldn't see the other driver perched ten feet above my helmet, but I can imagine his fury.

When I felt I was a few feet clear of him, I cut in and had the misfortune to have my front ten-inch wheel just glance off one of Britain's effective, but infamous, reflector lane marker studs, 'cats eyes', they are called. The tires lost their miniscule road-holding capability with the result that rider and Vespa did a seventy-yard slide on that wet asphalt surface in the path of the monster truck. The driver managed to stop inches from the 'Kamikaze-like' scooter operator.

I won't even try to write down the vocabulary he used. It was not a pretty sight or sound. I got shakily to my feet, and with this evidence of my surprise survival, he roared off north. It was amazingly quiet after he left. The bike had been well protected by the protruding ends of the suitcase and box. Each of these items showed significant abrasions which would prove the end of their usefulness, but the Vespa hadn't a scratch.

The much-maligned helmet had done yeoman service, but I was appalled at the appearance of my left arm. The yellow nerves, red arteries and blue veins sprouting from the remains of the canvas sleeve were just as they had been portrayed in the bible of medical students, *Gray's Anatomy*. As my befuddled brain analysed this desperate situation, it slowly fathomed out that the squiggly colourful items were in fact the heating and communication wires of the flight suit, which for the most part, was still serviceable although there was now a new wet area that pooled into my left glove. I was able to continue my trip, shaken, but in one piece.

Another excursion on the Vespa was my own 'Tour de France,' with my cousin, Neilson, the next summer. We rode through the real Arc de Triomphe in Paris and did a dozen circuits round the Eiffel Tower until a perceptive gendarme gave us an unmistakeable hand signal that obviously meant B...off.

Our tour took us to some of the memorials at Vimy Ridge and other sites of the horrors of two world wars. We finally ended up camping on a beach at the Bay of Biscay. Our tent was next to a huge ex-army Bell tent, housing three or four generations of a French family. They were a wonderful group, friendly and tolerant of my use of Scottish-accented French. I got on especially well with the grandparents, whose interest in us, and patient struggle with my translation inadequacies, made them great fun to be with. Neilson's elbow-digging and stage-whispering interrupted frequently.

"Get with the program, Blair. Start hitting on these girls. Ah really fancy the wee black-haired one." In that environment, even the 'chick-magnet' attraction of the Vespa didn't work any magic on the young beauties.

A year later, after many near-squeak incidents with the wee bike and fourteen thousand miles on the clock, I parked the trusty Vespa in a shed at my home in Scotland while I jaunted off to the Orient for three years. It was still there, dustily waiting for me when I returned, seemingly oblivious of my blatant unfaithfulness. I had bought my second Vespa in Kuala Lumpur.

Adventures on the enlarged twelve-inch wheels of Vespa #2 ticked off another eighteen thousand miles of Vespa addiction. The tropical climate and 90° F temperatures of Malaya didn't necessitate the great flying suit's protection, but I doubt if its zipper would have fared any better in the monsoon downpours. The redeeming feature of bike travel 5° north of the Equator was the reliable self-drying of wind and heat within five minutes of the deluge.

Vespa #2 was in a whole new world of popularity. By the early sixties there were one-hundred thousand of these bikes in use in the Orient. Families of four would cling to the magic machines. Used as taxis, they also were used to transport everything from dogs, to lumber, to cages of chickens, goats, and sheep, to boxes of coconuts and even sheets of 4'x 8' plywood.

I had a few skirmishes with the military bureaucracy for my preference of semi-nude attire on the bike. That was just not up to colonial British Standards. The crash helmet hadn't migrated to that part of the world so I reverted to hatless mode, and very little clothing, to nurture my almost-all-over tan.

There were numerous memorable unscheduled dismount incidents where rider and machine parted ways so that over the three years both of us had a few scars to show for the miles. One occurred when a Malay Racer, a seven foot long snake, chose to stretch out to enjoy the sun, blocking my path on the narrow roadway. He declined notice of my hooting the horn and did not give right-of-way, causing an embarrassing heap of vehicle and driver piled up in the encroaching jungle paralleling the roadside.

On another occasion, returning late at night from a weekend lazing on the beaches of Penang Island, exhaustion overtook me halfway up the forty mile tortuous mountain road to the British Military Hospital, Cameron Highlands. I stopped for a rest, set the bike up on its parking stand and slouched against the seat. Anxious about the residual fuel in the one gallon capacity tank, I switched off the engine and consequently the lights went off. The blackness must have qualified as stygian and the silence was absolute. My imagination conjured up an encroaching plethora of ghastly hungry animals: Snakes, leopards, wild boars, orang-utans, even centipedes, all undoubtedly carnivorous. With racing heart I was thrilled that V2 started on the first kick, and I gratefully followed its narrow headlight beam to the safety of the welcoming driveway leading up to my home away from home.

The Vespa (both #1 and #2) was the perfect mode of transportation for me as a young man finding his way in a new career, and with lots of new experiences. The lure of two-wheeled travel brought about V#3 and V#4 in Canada, and they gave me as much joy as had their predecessors. My total mileage reached nearly 40,000, which is a lot of turns of those little wheels on the Wee Vespa.

The Horizontal Man

*T*he very word, polio, still conjures up fear in the minds of those of us mature enough to have lived through the horrendous epidemic of the 1950's. Throughout recent history, the scourge of poliomyelitis had reared its ugly head with documented massive outbreaks in the 1800's and the suspicion that some of the plagues that annihilated huge tracts of civilization in earlier centuries may also have been that disease.

Defined as a central nervous system disorder, affecting the grey matter of the brain and certain columns of the spinal cord, it was commonly known as Infantile Paralysis. Although it had a predilection to affect children, it was not specific to that age group and also claimed adults as sufferers. Neither was it a disorder of ethnic or social class selectivity. Amongst its known celebrity sufferers, with varying major or minimal residual disability, are Franklin Roosevelt, Alan Alda, Neil Young and Mia Farrow.

The sheer numbers tell the story, with fifty-seven thousand reported cases in the USA in 1952. Polio was described as the most frightening public health problem of the post war era. Fortunately, after years of research, the Salk vaccine was introduced in 1955 as a safe and effective protection against the virus, and brought about the gradual drop in numbers of cases over the next two decades. North America was declared 'polio free', at last, in 1994.

Early in my physiotherapy training in 1957, amongst the seemingly endless list of things to learn about, polio lectures got everyone's full attention. A class of eighteen to twenty-five year olds, we could all remember vividly the fear and hushed discussions in our families during the post-war epidemics. There was understandable paranoia in those days when swimming pools were closed for the summer months, some schools closed as soon as the weather warmed up in May, and people avoided large gatherings.

You could hear a pin drop during the lectures about polio. There was still no awareness of how the disease spread, and with a polio ward in the adjacent Brook Hospital, with only a six foot high brick wall separating it from our football field, we all felt fearful of this silent killer.

It did little to lessen our anxiety to learn that polio's first onset included mild flu-like symptoms, headache, neck discomfort and stiffness, a mild cough, and slightly raised temperature. A single cough in that class precipitated a surreptitious neck forward bending test by the entire group to ascertain that the telltale diagnostic stiffness was absent.

Another classic early indicator was the information gleaned from observing the daily temperature of the patient. Over a week to ten days, the chart would show a slight rise for a day or two, followed by three or four days normal levels, then significantly greater increase over the next three or four days. The outline on the grid showed what was called a Dromedary chart, a small hump in front with a much larger hump further on, just like the two-humped camel whose name had been borrowed. Co-incidental to this revelation to our class there was a suspicious disappearance/theft of the thermometers from adjacent wards.

The delayed onset of the ensuing paralysis became more understandable as we learned the pathology of the condition. The muscles themselves weren't directly attacked by the virus but, to a lesser or greater degree, lost their ability to contract as the swelling and destruction of the brain and spinal cord cells inhibited their ability to send messages to the muscles.

Depending on the severity and location of the swelling, the extent of paralysis could provoke life-threatening situations if the muscles involved in swallowing and breathing was affected. The urgent availability of artificial mechanical breathing assistance for keeping the various swallowing and air vents open, were critical to the maintenance of life for those individuals.

Amongst the types of apparatus used to help those most severely disabled with their breathing was the memorably identifiable iron lung. It was a box-shaped piece of equipment, sadly often described as coffin-like. The patient's entire body was slid into the machine with only the head protruding from the end. A snug-fitting, rubber, air-seal collar ensured that alternating positive and negative pressures could be created within, compressing then expanding the thorax at fifteen to twenty cycles per minute, the normal breathing rate at rest. The iron lung was first introduced in 1928, following many experimental earlier vacuum type models. It is still in use around the world for those who have lost the ability to breathe unassisted due to severe paralysis.

It was with great relief that our hospital-based physiotherapy school group were early recipients of the Salk vaccine. Even so, there was still an aura of concern as we took turns working in the polio wards as part of our student rotation in 'hands-on' care of patients. In typical military logic, brawn rather than brain appeared to be the criteria for my selection for placement. "You're a big strong lad, you'll do," was all the information I got as I was led into the polio wing.

My first exposure to an iron lung and its resident inhabitant caught me speechless. I was introduced as 'Jock the Scot', and my saucer-sized eyeballs, look of disbelief, and silence spoke volumes. The motionless head at the end of the box had a beaming smile and the eyes swiveled to focus on me. "Hello Jock, nice to meet you. I'd shake your hand but mine are both a bit lazy this morning in here. I'm Tony," he chuckled. Automatically, my hand came up to the shake hand position, and then flopped embarrassedly as I realized the futility of that habitual reaction.

"I'm pleased to meet you." I struggled with the words.

"I'm glad you've found a big lad, Mrs. Wilson!" he said to my mentor, a qualified physiotherapist.

An auspicious and unforgettable moment in my career had taken place. It was the start of a daily hour of togetherness that lasted for the next three months, followed by sporadic visits for several years until time and distance separated us.

Tony had joined the Royal Air Force (R.A.F.) as a twenty year old and was selected for aircrew service. He was sent to the safe training area of the Canadian prairies where he went through the short but rigorous wartime flight school experience. He gained his wings as a qualified pilot the month the war ended in Europe.

His return to England was a dreadful anticlimax. Recently enlisted servicemen, even qualified pilots, were amongst the first group to be demobilized from the military. To make matters worse, the massive re-entry into civilian life of thousands of now redundant, yet very experienced, wartime flyers meant that Tony's employment prospects in civilian aviation were, as he so typically described it, "As hopeless as a snowball in hell."

Returning to his pre-enlistment work as a very junior sales executive, his occasional trips as a passenger to post war Europe were as close as he would ever get to his real career aspiration of being a pilot. Tony contracted 'the flu' on a visit to Paris two years after the war. Ten days later he was in the iron lung in that very same hospital where I met him ten years later.

Only someone with Tony's indomitable spirit could describe his permanent paralysis as he did. "I've been ever so lucky," he'd frequently tell listeners. "I can get out of the lung and sit up for a few hours each day and I can type with the two moving fingers of my right hand."

Tony had some minimal respiratory function which enabled him to huff and puff using what was described as frog breathing, a method of swallowing and forcing air into his lungs. For a daytime escape from the iron lung, he could survive for a few short hours struggling against all odds to be what he proudly proclaimed as 'normal'.

His leg musculature was only about five percent of what his 6'4" physique should have had, but the highlight of his day, he insisted, was his 'morning walk'. This was a rather exaggerated description of his ambulation capabilities, but none of us would ever have belittled his effort or denied him the right to describe it so.

With the help and guidance of Ron, a stalwart male ward assistant, I'd hoist Tony, all two hundred ten pounds of him, till he was standing, arms draped over our shoulders. I blink back a tear as I still hear Tony gasp out his orders in deference to my military uniform, perhaps recalling his brief life in the R.A.F.

"By the left, quick march!"

To describe the five-minute excursion as a walk or a march was a bit farfetched. We'd struggle to hold his body upright, and somehow help him flop one leg forward at a time, then wedge a knee against his to keep it straight, allowing forward motion as a team. The thirty yards to the end of the corridor was a seemingly endless journey.

Concerned always by his fast diminishing, labored breathing efforts, we'd do the turn around quickly and retrace our steps, getting more exhausted and a bit frantic to reach the target chair. Ron and I would be sweating profusely and Tony, eyes bulging, was speechless. Occasionally the effort by him was so great that we'd have to cry for help to get him lifted back into the iron lung for emergency re-oxygenation.

Even on those occasions, when he had revived enough to speak, the smile would again dominate and he'd gasp out, "That was the best damn run ever. Move over Roger Banister!" He'd glory in referring to that great athlete's recent breaking of the four-minute mile world record.

When he'd recuperated from the trauma of his morning walk, the irrepressible smile would return and Tony would attempt his next record-breaking venture. With the newspaper carefully flattened and clipped onto its tray, his pencil strapped to his only two minutely mobile fingers, he'd attack the Daily Telegraph crossword puzzle. It was heartbreaking, yet awe inspiring, to watch him scribble and scratch his way through the challenging mental stimulus of a timed successful completion of the puzzle. There was nothing wrong with Tony's brain.

At the end of my three-month rotation on the polio wing, I handed over the responsibility to the next physiotherapist with the 'big lad' prerequisites for the job. I'm sure he learned as much as I did of human perseverance from the enduring fortitude and unimaginably joyous spirit that I had seen in Tony.

It was to be almost three years before I'd again meet up with an iron lung and its unfortunate occupant. That particular machine may well have had a history related to its use by a polio sufferer ten years earlier in Malaya. The story is from an eloquent and heart-rending book called *The Horizontal Man,* by Paul Bates.

The pages tell the sad story of a twenty-year old British National Service Lieutenant in the jungles of Southeast Asia. They describe in detail the fortitude and perseverance of his changed life as a polio patient, and his way of dealing with the resultant disability from the disease. He overcame the limitations of a hospitalized stay, in an iron lung, and how, through the use of ongoing advances in technology, achieved a relatively independent life in his own home. It is a story of courage, determination and acceptance of challenges. I recommend, *The Horizontal Man* as being well worth the search to find a copy of the 1973 book.

My particular second experience involving an iron lung also happened in Malaya, seven thousand miles from the Brook Hospital in London. As so often occurred in the military service, it all started with a phone call. The hospital Commanding Officer on the line was always a scary experience. Either I'd been guilty of some grievous shortcoming in performing my allotted tasks, or worse still it was about some indiscretion that I'd hoped was overlooked, or the 'old man' (the C.O. was forty-five) had some devious challenge for me.

Without preamble he said, "Sergeant Farish, do you know anything about iron lungs?" I was silent for a moment while I tried to guess the potential ulterior motive of the question, so got the impatient sequel, "Well. Do you?"

Finally answering, I told him that I'd worked with them in London for three months. I failed to mention that I'd helped to get Tony out of and back into the contraption but hardly knew anything about the workings.

"Right," he said, "get on to that damned bike of yours and be at B.M.H. Taiping tomorrow night. They are having a terrible struggle with their machine."

I had neither time nor inclination to ask for more details. It didn't seem a good moment to push my luck. I'd had communications with him in the recent past, in particular with reference to the aforesaid, 'damned bike'. He meant of course, my beloved Vespa scooter, and more to the point, my flagrant disregard of the required dress code.

It was a standing order that British Servicemen leaving the hospital compound would be properly dressed. That meant in neat and tidy uniform or, if in civilian garb, long stockings to knee level, shorts down to knee level and a tidy, pressed shirt with no lurid insignia or pictures. It was all a vestigial remnant of days of the Raj.

Leaving camp on my Vespa (no helmet in those days) I always made sure I was appropriately attired, till I reached a local village half a mile down the road. There official dress was neatly folded and preserved in the bike's pannier and I was denuded to the scantiest of briefs. How else could I have achieved my much-envied almost all over tan?

Not willing to incur further wrath from the great man, I managed to squeeze a little further information from my pal who was the C.O.'s chief clerk, the original recipient of the call from Taiping, some two hundred miles north. The news was that they had a seriously ill polio patient, with some respiratory paralysis, who required the assistance of the iron lung, probably last used ten years earlier by the aforementioned Lieutenant.

At a guess, I'd be gone for two or three weeks so suitably attired (temporarily), I set off at dawn next day. The tan got a real boost for the first three hours, about a hundred miles, then I had to concede that I'd be fried if I didn't cover up a bit. While enjoying the trip for the most part, aside from a super scare from a six-foot python reluctant to concede the road to me, I pondered over the dilemma ahead. How did one switch on an iron lung?

After the six hour ride, the last half hour through a monsoon deluge, I was drying off in my room when a disgruntled Sergeant barged in unannounced. "You took your blooming time to get here!" I took no offence, seeing his Royal Electrical and Mechanical Engineers (R.E.M.E) shoulder patch. He was 'manna from heaven', an expert. My worries were over. "It took me four hours to get that lung to work properly," he said.

"Really," I answered, "I've never had a problem with them."

The patient was due to be installed in the lung next morning, so he and I went along that evening to do a final checkup on the machine. After a couple of beers later in the mess, I conceded my total ignorance of the workings of the apparatus. It cost me dearly because every time he and I met thereafter I heard, "You owe me!"

Next morning, with undeserved confidence thanks to my R.E.M.E pal, I met the patient. She was a lovely twenty-two year old Australian, named Jenny, whose husband was in the Air Force serving further north in Butterworth. She too had had 'the flu' for almost a week before the gradual onset of paralysis pointed to a more calamitous diagnosis.

As her respiratory function steadily became more impaired, the medical team determined that she needed the iron lung for survival. As we gradually coaxed her into that horrible machine, and despite indications that after the acute phase of the disease, subsiding swelling in her brain might allow restoration of independent breathing, she was extremely fearful.

My treatment for Jenny at that stage was twice daily visits to try to dislodge secretions that threatened to congest her lungs.

Additionally, through the side portals with their air lock rubber vents, I moved her legs and arms to prevent joint stiffening and muscle shortening caused by her inactivity. It was the only time I ever treated a patient in the early stages of paralysis from polio, and it gave me great satisfaction to be entrusted with that important part of the treatment. On my journey south after the return of the resident physiotherapist two weeks later, I recall feeling great joy at the privilege my profession had offered me.

Three months later, being recalled to do another two weeks locum at Taiping, I was thrilled to have the opportunity to again see Jenny. She was out of the iron lung but having intensive rehabilitation to get her walking again. She'd been fortunate to have considerable recovery of muscle strength. Her unassisted breathing ability was almost normal and she was at the stage of needing a frame walker to stand up. Over the two weeks she progressed further, but had an understandable fear of falling.

It was a wonderful moment when I coaxed her along a corridor, encouraging her as she used the walker for support. "Don't leave me!" she implored, as I walked behind her.

I cajoled her to keep going. "I'm right behind you," I lied. When she was ten short steps ahead of me, I said, "OK, let's turn around."

She carefully shuffled around, and only the delight in her face as she saw how far she'd gone, solo, cancelled out the blistering expletives that emitted from that pretty Aussie mouth. She finally forgave me as we hugged when she made the unassisted ten-step return journey.

It wasn't difficult to trace that moment of triumph to other earlier courageous walks at the side of an unforgettable patient, Tony, who will always be for me, that 'Horizontal Man' of my training days.

I've Been Everywhere Man!

I've been everywhere, man,
I've been everywhere, man,
Across the deserts bare man,
I've breathed the mountain air man,
Of travel I've done my share, man
I've been everywhere.

*A*lthough the original lyrics were written by Geoff Mack in 1959, mentioning over ninety known and unheard of places in Australia, the song itself has been everywhere. Local renditions have sprouted in Japan, South America, Germany, Spain and many other unlikely locations. Of course, since the early 1960's, it has translated conveniently to the vast open spaces of Canada and the U.S.A. It was ably vocalised by our very own Hank Snow and Stompin' Tom Connors, and given an American flavour by such legends as Johnny Cash and Willie Nelson.

I'd contribute my own version but Auchtermuchty, Killicrankie, Kirkudbright, Ecclefechan and Yell combined with Ballachulish are hard to rhyme together. Add this to the Scottish brogue that I revert to at the very mention of the land of my birth, and it is unlikely the result would be pleasing.

Suffice to say, my visits to some thirty countries in the past half century, allows me to legitimately proclaim that, indeed, I've been everywhere. Many of the varied locations I visited were only brief, one or two day stopovers, each intriguing and memorable to me, but too numerous to detail adequately in these pages. The more prolonged visits, in locations that influenced me, are described. Many were postings, or journeys to postings, and some were vacations, but there was another type of travel that related to my training as a physiotherapist.

Armies the world over are renowned for their penchant for moving personnel to unexpected new locations, with seemingly total disregard for the wishes of the individual serving member. Those often abrupt postings played havoc with the plans and relationships of those being moved. Such was the case when I received notice only twelve hours before being sent from the physiotherapy school at Woolwich, to Chester some two hundred miles north.

"It's just for two months and you'll get superb training experience at the Army Medical Rehabilitation Unit (A.M.R.U.). It's run mostly by staff of the Physical Training Corps, amazing chaps, specialists all. I suppose you'll travel on that Vespa of yours, so set off early tomorrow morning. Good luck!" Brevity of command was the style of Arthur Smith, the school principal. My thoughts or responses were uninvited.

Half an hour of inquiry in the canteen gave me the good, bad and ugly of my future temporary home. It was hard to distinguish truth from fabrication from those who had 'been there, done that', but I was excited by the prospects of a new learning environment, and for two months could survive the element of greatest concern outlined by one reporter: "Gee, what a dump. There are a thousand blokes there and not half a dozen birds," was his mournful analysis of the male to female ratio of staff in the unit at Chester. High on the plus side was the prospect of being able to visit some of the great football stadiums at nearby Liverpool, Everton and Blackpool. I might even get to see (the future Sir) Stanley Mathews mesmerising the opposing team with his dazzling dribbling skills.

Getting to Chester from Woolwich offered another exciting escapade, a chance to ride on the recently opened M-1, the first motorway in the UK. Vehicles using that highway had to be able to achieve fifty miles per hour, and the Vespa satisfied that requirement, just, with its fifty-three miles per hour maximum speed.

At Chester, the A.M.R.U. was housed on a war-time Air Force base. The former aeroplane hangars had been converted into massive gymnasiums. All accommodations for patients and staff were in clusters of wooden huts, each sleeping about twenty. It was the 'finishing school' for patients sent from army hospitals all over the UK. These patients had undergone earlier care from surgical and medical specialists, and had advanced to where they needed only graduated exercise programs to ready them for 'fully-fit' return to their individual regiment or bases.

The five hundred or so patients were categorized into their area of disability such as hips, shoulders, knees, spines, and further divided into grading levels denoting their advancement through individual classes. 'Legs' would be formed into groups of ten to fifteen patients, 'non-weight bearing', 'partial-weight bearing', and 'full-weight bearing', with an instructor for each class.

As the only physiotherapy student on the base, I had a schedule of activity designed so that I'd follow a different class-level each day. In the morning I'd join the patients following the instructor's exercise regime. By afternoon I was let loose, under his strict supervision, to lead that group's program. It was the most intense participation I could have imagined, and the instructors were superb. Without exception they were as Arthur Smith had described them, specialists in their fields.

Fortunately I'd started at the early rehab levels and had an opportunity to advance through the levels gradually. By the last few days of my two months' stay I was able to participate in the final 'arduous training' classes designed specifically for those returning to infantry and special activity services such as parachute and commando units. I came to realise that being a very fit athlete in the medical corps fell far short of the physical requirements of some of the elite regiments. My earlier expectation of jaunts off to football matches, or prowling around the ancient walled city of Chester, or visiting the high spots of Liverpool before the Beatles became famous, was a non-starter due to my physical exhaustion at the end of each work day. But looking back, I consider those two months at Chester a major positive influence in my training, and things learned there stayed with me though my fifty-year career.

I spent two months back in the school in Woolwich before yet another decision was sprung on me. "You'll get a valuable, two-month learning experience, starting tomorrow, at Millbank Medical Hospital." In central West London not far from Buckingham Palace, Millbank was considered to be modern, opened in 1905, but still built on the Nightingale-pattern with cavernous wards accommodating forty beds in each. As in the Royal Herbert Hospital, the huge windows were always slung open, regardless of outside temperature or London smog fogs.

The majority of the patients were from local units such as the ceremonial duty rotations of the Guards and Household Cavalry. However, the proximity to the war office made it the convenient medical centre for the upper ranks of 'Officers and Gentlemen'. This offered a mature group of patients seldom seen in other military hospitals, where the clientele was customarily on the low side of eighteen to thirty-five years. Few Generals were less than fifty.

Another fascinating patient group seen in Millbank Hospital were the real 'old soldiers', residents of the nearby Chelsea Pensioners' Home. These wonderful old gents, mostly First World War veterans and some who had even soldiered in the Boer War, were in a class to themselves. When they were up and about they proudly wore their distinctive medal-bedecked scarlet tunics. They deserved, and got, respect from everyone they encountered.

Again, due to their ages, the old soldiers provided a spectrum of ailments that I had not previously seen, having predominately treated young patients. Diabetes, strokes, heart attacks, cancers, lung disorders, fractured hips, bed sores, amputations required for gangrene, and a myriad of other conditions afflicting the elderly were common. Even just talking with those very special old gentlemen was a learning experience for me, a nineteen year old.

Recognition of all these Old Warriors was highlighted in a wonderful tribute. Chelsea Football Club attached a small scarlet ribbon on the sleeves of their team shirts in the 2010-2011 season.

Along with the amazing work experience it offered, my two month interlude at Millbank was unique in another way. There was a shortage of staff accommodations in the barracks in central London, so temporarily-attached people such as myself were invited to find civilian housing where possible. I'd started my posting at Millbank by commuting the fifteen miles from Woolwich by Vespa, which seemed like an exciting prospect at the time. Very soon, the almost suicidal rush-hour traffic became much less attractive, as I was jostled morning and evening by double-decker buses, taxis, trucks and other-inconsiderate road-users.

Asking around amongst my new fellow staff members I got a line on a nearby shared flat at a rate well covered by the living-out allowance paid by the army. Sight unseen I sent on the first week's advance of rent with a chum already living there. Next evening, I located the place, parked my kit-loaded Vespa on the sidewalk near the eight steps leading up to the front door of the four-story, early Victorian row housing unit. I rang the bell.

Through the mail slot, a booming voice demanded, "What do you want?" I explained my situation and after a few seconds a woman opened the door and inspected me. She spied my suitcase and kit bag and said, "There's only one locker and you'll have to chain that bike to the fence." She pointed to the six foot high railings covering the downstairs windows. In Sergeant Major mode she continued, "The doors are locked and chained at 11 pm, no noise, no drinking, and no female visitors on this property."

Risking loss of the Vespa, having not anticipated the 'you need to chain it up' factor, I hauled my luggage up to the top attic room that had three army beds and lockers, and less floor space than a conventional barrack room. I jammed my worldly possessions into the locker, wedged the suitcase and bag under the bed, and determined that there was a lock for the door. I scurried down to street level to rescue my providentially still un-stolen Vespa, then toured around for miles to find a hardware store that sold chains and locks at astronomical prices.

Just before the specified curfew time I immobilised the bike and entered the gloomy flat. My fellow roommates didn't materialise, but the shared unsanitary bathroom sink and toilet helped me make a quick decision on the impermanence of my stay. I had to scoot off to work early next morning having had a sleepless night. I couldn't believe that a fire station, ambulance garage and police depot could all be within fifty yards of that flat, or at least that's what it had seemed during the night. Right after work I was back packing gear, loading up the Vespa for the return trip to Woolwich. I chose the more attractive option of potential rush-hour suicide instead of that accommodation. I can still hear the land lady's very hearty laughter when I asked for a refund of my week's rent. I don't make a habit of announcing that I once lived in a flat in London's trendy West End, for fear of having to divulge the whole story.

Back at school in Woolwich after experiencing so much practical training at Millbank, it was immersion into academics twenty-four/ seven. I settled into the scholastic routine for a few months, almost anticipating the next short-notice posting. It wasn't long coming. One day, almost as an aside, when I met the boss in the corridor I got the ten-word notification. "Ah Farish, they need you in Aldershot, tomorrow. Good luck." It was the first time in my army career that I'd been told I was 'needed'. Things were looking up. After all I was in the third year of my training, though sometimes that seniority was over looked.

Vespa, suitcase and pack-sack equipped, I departed early next morning. Aldershot, 'Home of the British Army', was the training base for the Parachute Regiment, and a home-training depot for the Ghurkhas. It was a place where at least one pub beaten-up, or motorcycle-injured, or sports-fractured soldier is admitted to the hospital every day of the year.

The two new chevrons on my sleeve made quite a difference to my arrival and barrack comforts. I was shown where I could safely park my bike in the hospital compound, and given a friendly welcome. Getting some administrative details sorted out, the chief clerk poked his head out of his office. "Oh there you are, Corporal Farish, we've been expecting you. You're centre forward on the unit football team tomorrow afternoon." Once again, football was the acceptance ticket. I felt a bit anxious as I reported for work next morning, to begin my stay there by asking for the afternoon off to play football.

"No problem," the Staff Sergeant, head of the department, assured me. "But watch out, those Royal Artillery guys are pretty rough."

He was right, the opponents were mean. I settled in hoping to make a good first impression on my teammates. All went well when I scored a goal, but I paid for it moments later by being foul tackled. I hobbled around for the last five minutes, but felt vindicated when we won the game.

Aldershot gave me a prospective on the size of the army. The hospital itself had a capacity of seven hundred beds that were fully occupied most of the time. There were about twenty football and rugby pitches. These seemed to be constantly in use as the half-dozen regiments, training depots, major stores, and administration sections encouraged their teams to be involved in extremely competitive encounters. Occasionally a group of us would catch the Aldershot Town professional football games at weekends, and witness the high calibre skills of their players including two R.A.M.C. National Servicemen who also led our hospital team midweek.

Work was busy and interesting. There were three older army physiotherapists and two qualified civilians, all with loads of experience, so it was a great mentoring department.

The two months flashed by and yet another notable experience came to an end. Aldershot was added to the long list of special locations that validate my assertion that, "I've been (nearly) everywhere, man."

Tidworth Military Hospital

*G*etting a call to the office was seldom something anticipated with joy, especially on Fridays. We knew that was the day the Principal of our training school at Woolwich, Arthur Smith, wanted to depart promptly at four o'clock to beat the rush hour traffic on his journey to his family home in Netly near Southampton. He still held a grudge about the school's move from that location to Woolwich two years earlier. And in the last week of November, 1960, three of us, the senior students, had special cause for trepidation. We had just completed the final civilian exam in our physiotherapy training, held at the austere Medical Examination Centre in Russel Square, central London, and were awaiting results.

I watched the other two finalists take their turns entering the inner sanctum of the office, each with fear and trembling. As I waited my turn, it was of little consolation that each had returned a changed person, floating out in the glory of their 'pass' mark. I did the required gentle rap on the door, waited the customary five seconds purposeful delay before the command, "Enter," was heard. Arthur's usually cluttered desk was clean except for three letter folders, two set aside and one glaringly the centre of his attention. My knees nearly gave way as he slowly opened the file. The single sheet inside, the tiny print upside down from my viewpoint, didn't give me a hint of the message it contained.

He maintained a dour look for a few seconds, then broke into a big smile and said, "You passed, well done," and gave me a hearty hand shake. Unlike today's protracted graduation ceremonies, that was it. "I've phoned the quarter master to confirm that you'll be in to pick up your Sergeant's stripes," he added. The new promotion was automatic with passing that final exam, when one became a member of the Chartered Society of Physiotherapy.

"Oh, by the way, you are posted to Tidworth. The chief clerk will have your rail ticket ready. I believe you take the 8:00 am train tomorrow. Good luck."

I bounded out, ecstatic, and just a little surprised that I'd really done it. I'd achieved my dream, and the recruiting Sergeant's prediction three years earlier. My chosen career wish had come true.

It seemed I was the last to learn of the exam result. The whole administrative office congratulated me as I picked up my train ticket and posting order, already typed up. My three chevrons were on the counter as I entered the stores. In the main hospital corridor a Queen Alexandra nursing Staff Sergeant hooked me by the arm and 'ordered' me to take her to the Sergeants' Mess, where I had to buy everyone in attendance the customary celebratory pint. It's amazing how fast news travels, and how many members can suddenly appear in a Sergeants' Mess, at the chance of a free drink at the new boy's expense. I tried to escape but my escort of the moment had come prepared, and she took a purposely inordinate time to sew the new stripes on my tunic.

Hours later, my entire worldly possessions were bundled into a kit bag and suitcase and I was ready to set off for new pastures the next morning. I rushed down to the cook-house at 6:00 am to get an early breakfast, only to be rudely banished by the cook. "No Sergeants allowed in here," he said with a smile. I almost had to look at my new shoulder patches to see if it was true.

Nothing could go wrong that morning. Number 89 bus to the railway station was empty, there was ample room on the train to Charing Cross, the tube train glided along to Waterloo, and I had an empty compartment to myself all the way to Andover. The trip went so smoothly that I snoozed and was jerked awake by the guard's whistle. I bailed out frantically, landing in a heap with my luggage.

Tidworth Military Hospital, on the edge of the Salisbury Plain, is just twenty miles from one of Britain's oldest archaeological treasures, Stonehenge. Dating back some four thousand years, the great sandstone and dolerite stones dominate the undulating chalk downs of Southern England. They stand, forty-ton stones, apparently oblivious to the passing tourist hordes and the prowling tanks, artillery and tens of thousands of troops on the training ranges nearby.

The hospital, built in 1907, had three hundred beds at its peak, although early on had been augmented by a massive, twelve hundred-bed tent hospital to provide treatment for returning WWI injured. When I was there in the early 1960's Tidworth offered acute surgical and medical care for local service personnel and their families. However, it had diminished to a mere one hundred-bed capacity as the majority of more serious cases were sent to the wider range of specialist services in Aldershot.

My time in Tidworth, although I didn't know it on arrival, was to be only six months, but that was time enough for me to figure out that I still had a lot to learn. I got settled in with my luggage to a pleasant, small, private room and ventured into the mess for supper. I was welcomed by the living-in members, mostly National Service pharmacists, radiographers, opticians and male registered nurses. Later, more of the married personnel arrived for the Saturday night socializing. I'd become involved in a snooker match and took off my tunic to facilitate some spectacular shot. Learning experience #1 at Tidworth --removing my jacket showed only Corporal's stripes for all to see. That glaring evidence of my very recent promotion cost me dearly in a full-house penalty, drinks all round.

Work was interesting and varied in the small department with a two physiotherapist quota. We were situated adjacent to the casualty department and junior doctors there would often invite our opinions when assessing patients with musculo-skeletal problems. That was a unique learning opportunity for me.

My arrival, very early in December was seen as a turn of good fortune by the other Sergeants, as I was immediately scheduled for the much disliked regimental duties over the upcoming Christmas and New Year holidays. My inexperience showed blatantly on those occasions, as I was over zealous in identifying and accosting staff overindulging while on duty. Dragging one slightly inebriated orderly before the powers that be, I was asked what had happened to my 'spirit of the season' of good will to all men, and was told to turn a blind eye to trivial matters. The learning curve was getting steeper. Eventually I learned to balance official duty with 'live and let live'.

The variety of patients from such a wide spectrum of regiments and services was fascinating. One memorable occasion started with my treatment of a six-foot-six Sergeant Major from a Guards' unit. I shrank back when this colossus arrived, intimidated by both his rank and dimension. I was only twenty-one. He was in his forties, and king of all he surveyed, the senior non-commissioned officer in charge of six hundred-fifty men. While other patients would stomp in uncaringly out of the wet, he made a real fuss of wiping his size fourteen boots on the mat at the door. He had just settled into a cubicle for treatment on his back, when the department door was flung open by an impatient patient. He too was a Guards' officer, Lieutenant, the Earl of Somewhere, and definitely full of his own importance. Before I could even speak he demanded loudly that he wanted his next appointment time changed to an 8:00 am visit. I was about to accede when a voice boomed from behind the curtain. "That's my parade time, Lieutenant, and you wouldn't want to miss that would you?"

The self-important kid recognised the voice instantly. "Oh dear, I just never thought of the parade, Sgt Major." And that was the end of that communication.

Sports were a big part of the entertainment of the troops, especially football. The hospital had a superb team despite the low numbers of men in the unit. It helped that we had three National Servicemen who were professionals in major league teams, and so we did well against teams from the regiments. One memorable, rain-drenched afternoon we were leading 3-1 at half time. Both teams stood around in the wet, nibbling the traditional half-time slice of orange. My former patient, the Guards' R.S.M. suddenly came striding across the field, seemingly getting larger with each step. He didn't hear the whisper amongst our opposition players, "Lookout, here comes god." They, however, definitely heard his non-ambiguous suggestions of the dire consequences that awaited them if they didn't win. Needless to say they beat us 5-3.

Despite unrelenting terrible weather that winter, the isolation of the small hospital community at Tidworth fostered a lot of fun in the gyms, canteens, and messes. Bands formed, comedy groups put on skits, and there seemed to be many diverse activities to keep up the morale. Personalities emerged to organise guided tours to Stonehenge, Salisbury Cathedral and other historic sites.

The six months went past very quickly. Nurtured by supportive fellow staff members, I improved my professional skills and regimental experience. I also gained confidence through the amazing camaraderie there. I was sad to leave Tidworth Military Hospital.

Off to the Orient

*M*y return to the R.A.M.C. depot at Crookham, as a Sergeant, albeit recently promoted and still only twenty-one, was a far cry from the unforgettable prior experience there when I was a raw recruit just a few years earlier. I'd had the foresight to have a haircut, with short back and sides, but nothing like the scalping needed for my earlier visit.

My single-occupant room in the Sergeants' Mess was a palatial accommodation compared to the forty square feet of floor space I'd been allocated in the thirty-person squad barrack-room. The mess dining room even had white tablecloths, although we still had to collect our food buffet style.

Even my first meeting with the Sergeant Major, though still tinged with a suspicion of fear, was an almost human contact. "Just passing through are you, Sergeant?" he said as he stopped by where I was sitting. I reflexively almost leapt to attention but he allayed my fears. He seemed to have shrunk. I thought I remembered him as eight foot tall and four foot wide. We chatted, almost man-to-man. He'd been to Malaya years earlier and assured me I'd enjoy my posting there. "It's pretty quiet there now," he assured me. "It wasn't always that way." He didn't elaborate, but I'd learn later that it had been a rather dangerous country in the 50's, a mini Vietnam, jungle warfare for British and Commonwealth military personnel.

I spent only two days getting 'kitted out' for tropical climes. The old soldiers gave out liberal warnings and cautions, and on their advice, I jettisoned all superfluous personal clothing and artifacts. I felt my half-full kit bag had ample room for the new uniforms and items I'd wear once we shipped out and got into the heat of the Mediterranean.

My visit to the clothing store shattered the delusion that I had room to spare and was a reminder of my first issue of army kit. On this occasion, I had to collect the OG's, or olive green, uniforms suitable for wear in the tropics. The earlier hint of the past dangers of Malayan service made the jungle-green camouflage colour take on an ominous connotation.

I had forgotten the army's lackadaisical system of selecting garment sizes. My suspicions increased when the young stores-man did his total analysis of my clothing measurements with a microsecond glance, before he turned and started grabbing items off the shelves behind him. As in the past, the first item was a green poncho that he kindly spread out on the counter. Thereafter, he went into a much practiced, monotonous chant as he travelled along, intoning, "OG shirts, four; OG under vests, four; OG slacks, four; OG shorts, four; Puttees, OG, pairs, two." At the mention of those ankle-wrapping straps, I was appalled that they were still issued, items that had been part of a soldier's kit in the Crimean War, but I didn't have the opportunity to express my disbelief.

With almost a pirouette, he dumped the heap onto the poncho and swung back to start again. "Dress white tunic, one; dress white slacks, one; dress white shorts, one; long stockings white, pairs, two; OG stockings, long pairs, four." Again he paused, swiveled and dumped.

The heap of clothing was becoming immense. I thought anxiously of the small space I had remaining in my kit bag to accommodate the 'few items' I'd been told I'd need to carry. The list went on and on. The heap grew. As if to get his last bit of entertainment, he planted handfuls of small items on the pile. "OG buttons, with rings twenty-six; OG water bottle, one; Sergeants' stripes OG three pairs; Sergeants' stripes gold one pair; OG belt, one." With a flourish he slammed down a list of equipment with a hundred pre-scribbled ticks indicating the transfer of these items from his shelves to my personal possession. He held out a ballpoint pen and stabbed the papers with his other index finger at the dotted line where the huge 'X' awaited my signature.

He lorded over his store-man position of power and was not remotely fazed by the disparity in our rank or age. He was waiting for his moment of cruel joy as he watched me try to wrap everything into the poncho. As the buttons fell at my feet he made no effort to help. Matters occurring on the distant side of his countertop were not in his jurisdiction.

I struggled back to the Sergeants' Mess and laid everything out in my room. It covered the bed and every horizontal surface. It took no time to realize that there was a discrepancy in volume between available space and goods needing to be transported. After inquiring around, an empty, much-battered suitcase appeared, seeming to just cry out for a new owner. I embraced the poor waif and painted over the previous owner's template with my name, rank and number. Even with this new space allotment it would be touch-and-go.

Further inquires about what else I might jettison brought forth a great disappointment. I'd had a brain wave. No one in their sane mind would take an army great coat to the tropics. They were huge, heavy and had been lifesavers in the mud at Passchendaele. Their German counterpart was clearly designed for skirmishes such as the siege of Stalingrad. Closer to home these coats were highly valued by Highland Regiments in desolate stances on the bulwarks of Edinburgh Castle in a Scottish gale. The great coat could be disposed of. Not wanting to leave incriminating evidence, I bundled it into an unrecognizable shape. I was wedging it into a garbage bin when a passing colleague spied my subterfuge. He was a fellow Scot, so his warning wasn't subject to misinterpretation.

"They'll kill ye if ye don't pack that wi' ye!" he admonished. He went on to explain that there had been hell to pay, years earlier, when a regiment serving in Malaya had been hustled off, almost overnight, to join the fray in Korea in 1951. The snow-covered hills near the 38th parallel were decidedly frigid environments for the tropic-kitted-out new arrivals. Consequently, ten years later, great coats were a number one priority on the list of what needed to be taken to Singapore, a base straddling the equator.

My kit bag and newfound suitcase literally bursting at the seams, everything was wedged in. Anxious, and anticipating a disaster, I carefully placed my belongings on the truck leaving for the railway station en route to Southampton. A few stragglers, similarly overloaded with equipment, crashed their gear on top of mine. I shuddered and hoped for the best.

Fleet Station, the station closest to Aldershot and Crookham, was chockablock with bodies. Somehow, everybody got on the train. Baggage blocked doorways and corridors but we all survived the two hour journey, to be deposited on the docks. Red Cap military police assembled the groups of overloaded bodies into lines that stretched into the distance. We shuffled forward in the midday heat, sweating and swearing, and finally got to the ramps leading up onto the deck of the gleaming white troop-carrying ship, the Oxfordshire.

There were still a few hurdles to overcome. As we reached the top of the steep incline, a harassed Corporal tried to document our arrival. "Name, rank, last three numbers!" he'd yell, and then search for that individual amongst his reams of paper.

"McDonald, Rifleman, 075," replied the young Scot ahead of me. There was an inevitable delay as the man with the list tried to discern which of his five McDonald's was facing him. That was a likely occurrence when a battalion of Highland Infantry is boarding ship.

"Farish, Sergeant, 550!" I shouted, reaffirming that I was the one and only of my tribe. With my name recorded, I was allowed to pass.

I hadn't made it three steps on deck when a voice bellowed, "Get those bloody boots off!" The Chief Petty Officer was apparently unhappy that my metal-studded army boots might injure his recently scrubbed decks. I joined the struggling heap of humanity perched on our individual pyramids of personal belongings as each of us removed the offending boots. It wasn't the time to discuss the added nuisance factor of further items that needed to be carried aboard.

With boots, precariously swinging by their tied laces, threatening to choke me, I tried to interpret the scribbles on the deck layout sheet I'd been handed. The ship was one hundred yards long, ninety feet wide and forty feet of it was below sea level. Deck G, Forward, Portside, Bunk 146, Upper, Locker 228, wasn't exactly easily identifiable on the 5" x 8" sheet. The 'map' was more intricate than the London underground, and the print microscopic.

Half an hour later, shins and skull bleeding from my inexperienced maneuvering down narrow stairways and through watertight four-foot high apertures, I found Bunk 146. I saw that 'Upper' was the topmost of three bunks, a mere twenty-four inches of vertical height below the ceiling. Naturally, the locker for my kit was about as far distant as possible from my bunk in that tomb of a sleeping quarter that I shared with ninety others.

After much more swearing, I finally located my canvas running shoes, plimsols as they were called. I'd thoughtlessly packed them at the bottom of my kit bag. It seemed ironic that I'd put them on thirty feet below the water level demarked by the line of the same name, the Plimsol Line, which indicated the safe maximum load-level of the ship.

Ascending to the top deck, by some obscure route that didn't seem to relate to my map, I joined the two thousand fellow voyagers about to bid farewell to England's 'Green and Pleasant Land'. There wasn't much green or pleasant to see in the dockyards of Southampton at that moment. The last straggling, reluctant debutants were dragging their worldly possessions aboard, Red Caps nipping at their heels like angry sheep dogs.

Eventually, a somber moment, the great ship's siren hooted. It signaled for many of us, the start of a three-year emigration. A scattering of relatives stood sadly on the waterfront waving flags, trying to hide their tears. Tiny tots waved to their daddies, just dots, somewhere high on the ships' rails. The Oxfordshire eased out slowly as the miniature tugs worked their magic.

No one left the open decks as we slowly picked up steam and moved down the estuary. Some of the old Navy hands pointed out the remains of Netley Military Hospital. It had seen better days since Queen Victoria had visited it a century earlier. It had served its country as asylum, surgical centre and, at the time of the final years of WWII, as the first homeland treatment centre for the wounded returning from the invasion of Europe.

Gradually, our ship took a westerly course leaving the shelter of the Isle of Wight. Turning into the English Channel proper was the signal for many of the troops to drown their sorrows, or celebrate, in the pubs and canteens onboard. After two pints, the rougher waters of the Bay of Biscay sent me trying again to navigate the labyrinth en route to the elusive Bunk 146. When I arrived, ages later, the airless cavern was already almost uninhabitable. I climbed up onto that top bunk and covered my head with the blanket to try to filter out the putrid stench. At 2:00 am, with stragglers from the bar making their final discordant rendition of, "I belong to Glasgow," I'd had as much as I could stand. Up, up and away, I fled, shrouded in a blanket for warmth, and found a somewhat sheltered corner on the open deck. It was far from comfortable. The seventeen-knot speed, and the roll and pitch, made sleep impossible, but the trade-off was breathable air.

Finally, turning east through the narrows at Gibraltar, we encountered heat, sun and the pleasant prospect of, at last, being off to the Orient!

POSH

Oh the posh, posh travelling life
The travelling life for me
First Class cabin, Captain's table and regal company.
Pardon the dust of the upper crust,
Fetch me a cup of tea.
Port out, Starboard home
Posh with a capital 'P'.

From Chitty, Chitty, Bang, Bang.

*T*he twenty thousand ton troop-ship, Oxfordshire, carried us through the eastern Atlantic for two days until we reached the Rock of Gibraltar. Passing between the 'Pillars of Hercules' into what had been the limit of the known world in ancient times, there was a communal sigh of relief at the prospect of calm sailing through the Mediterranean.

We had twenty-four days ahead of us on our 'cruise', sightseeing and taking in the history of the pink parts of the world map where Queen Victoria had stretched the British Empire far and wide. We started the 'sightseeing' part with a four-hour shore leave in Gibraltar. In those short four hours the lure of the tavern resulted in more than a few stragglers wobbling back aboard at the last minute.

Steaming off with Spain on the left, the port side, and in the distance the jagged peaks of Morocco to starboard, the transformation from Atlantic rough waters to calm sailing, was like night and day in comfort. It was also easy to imagine the origin of the old Victorian myth of the aristocrats and well-offs selecting the port side of the ship, outbound. That avoided the scorching heat that baked the southern starboard side of the ships as they made their way to India and other British possessions in the good old days.

It made little difference to me, as I had abandoned the almost uninhabitable sleeping Deck G with my allotted Bunk 146. I found a sheltered niche on the open upper deck and claimed it as my personal space for the rest of the voyage. I made furtive short-duration visits to my locker as infrequently as possible.

All the troops aboard had been allocated specific daily tasks, which, for the most part, involved two to three hour 'make-work' projects in the mornings. I reported to the ship's hospital as my delegated work place. Introducing myself to the ward master, an R.A.M.C. Warrant Officer, I was met with undisguised disappointment. He had been anticipating my presence aboard, assuming that I would bring with me some useable nursing experience to add to his half dozen permanent staff running the ship's hospital.

He didn't mince words to express his frustration. "What bloody good is a physiotherapist in a ship's emergency medical centre?" By good fortune, he was a Scot, so seemed mollified that we'd at least speak the same language. "Oh well," he sighed," I'll put you in charge of the hospital cleaning gang. You'll know more than the ten infantrymen you will be babysitting. Have fun." I had the suspicion that there was something hidden in that statement. He knew something I didn't from his four years at sea, right since the launch of the Oxfordshire from the Glasgow dockyards in 1957.

I got my gang that first day at sea, and they filled the bill of the proverbial motley crew. That group of Highland Light Infantry, rough and tough without exception, all viewed their new leader with evident disdain. I'm sure out in the battlefield they appreciated their medic, but there was no sign of the respect I'd hoped for at that first meeting. Rather, I could almost see glee as they took an exaggerated casual stance when I outlined what was expected from them.

Far from the eagle eye of their regiment's disciplinary hierarchy, the gleaming white corridors of the infirmary were about to be their playground it seemed. I knew I was in trouble. Dusting, washing and polishing the ship's decks had not been part of their basic training, although they found ways to entertain each other with their interpretation of what they had been told to do. Fortunately, each morning's saga was only for about two and a half hours. I bossed them, cajoled them, humoured them, and almost pleaded with them, and barely survived. The ward master seemed to enjoy my discomfort almost as much as my gang did. Finally taking pity on me, he took me into his little office, closed the door, sat me down and had a good chuckle.

"It's the same every time, the first couple of days, so don't feel too bad about not being able to handle those little creeps. Here's what you do. Go back out there as mad as hell and tell them that I've just blasted you." He gave a huge wink to reassure me, "Then tell them I'll be inspecting the finished job tomorrow." As I left, he gave a cheery wave, and then shouted for my squad's benefit, "If I find one speck of dust or a hair they'll be on the job for eight hours every day till we get to Singapore!"

I played the game. With mock, bursting-point anger, I lined them up in that narrow corridor, put on apoplectic crimson face, walked back and forward past their suddenly more soldierly stature, and read them the riot act. I was actually enjoying myself. Finally I dismissed them in a rather unprofessional manner. "Right, bugger off," I shouted. That was their kind of language.

To my disbelief, as one man they answered, "Yes Sergeant!" and set off in some semblance of military order. The ward master came out of his cubbyhole when they'd left. "That was quite a performance. That should do the job." Next morning I purposely arrived five minutes late on station. My boys were busy at work and gave me an unprecedented, semi-sincere, "Morning Sarg." All was well on the high seas.

We passed Malta on our port bow, another of Queen Vic's pink islands. This was a place of questionable past history, belying today's deserved reputation as a delightful tourist Mecca. During World War II that isolated stronghold had been savaged by Axis' bombing. The barrage was an attempt to dislodge the embattled British servicemen who were there to retain Malta as a strategic port of call for Allied shipping. For courageous defense and resistance, the Maltese, deserving of Royal recognition, received the George Cross Island Medal for valor. Much earlier, Malta's population had been traumatized when the empire-seeking Brits wrestled it from Napoleon's grasp. As a further claim to infamy as a historical black spot, that speck in the middle of the Mediterranean was also the place where St. Paul is said to have been ship wrecked. With my gang under some pretence of cooperation, we sailed on, oblivious of the island's historic past.

As our journey continued, I soon realized that, over time, fifteen hundred troops will have their fun, usually at the expense and discomfort of whomever their closest target of the day happened to be. And such a target, as if in answer to their prayers, appeared in the form of the deck duty officer. He was a National Serviceman, a very new Second Lieutenant, not a day over nineteen, and still of pimply complexion. To add to his misfortunes, he had foolishly let it be known that he was the offspring of one of the great chocolate manufacturing families of England.

On deck, this poor young fellow's job was supervising a mass of half-naked bodies all vying for the best spot for a prefect suntan. Each day, once the troops had attended, if not performed, their morning work, the decks became a blaze of pink shoulders and backs. The standard pallor of Brits, and especially the Scots, (tanning is uncommon in the mists of the Highlands from September till July, and even then midges discourage nudity) was a great incentive for the lads to take advantage of the mid-day Mediterranean sun to try to get the best-bronzed tan.

The Second Lieutenant took it upon himself to make a point of advising the prostrate sunbathers. "Sunburn is a self-inflicted injury, and is punishable in the military," he informed them voiced in his upper class accent. Had he pronounced this gem of wisdom only once, accurate as it was, he might have escaped the eventual rancor. He was, however, relentlessly persistent in offering the advice. As a result, his presence inevitably produced, in stage whisper, "Here comes the Chocolate Soldier." His ears would pink-up even before some scallywag, primed by his pals would say, "Excuse me Lieutenant, Sir, do you think my sunburn's getting dangerous yet?" Poor kid, I felt sorry for him, perhaps still a bit raw from being similarly traumatized by my cleaning party.

I didn't realize that more fun at my expense was yet to come. As we approached Port Said, the ship had gone a whole seven days without being repainted. That was quite unusual for a military sea-going vessel. My gang was told to have the cleaning chores completed in one hour, then as a reward presumably, they'd be out in the sunshine painting the ship's rails. Duly equipped with buckets of white paint and brushes, they started smearing another coat of paint on the existing half-inch thick mass on the rails. I was quite relaxed as I supervised my crew in work that wasn't exactly high tech or onerous.

I should have suspected that the tranquility wouldn't last. It took all of ten minutes before one of my men reported that his paintbrush had fallen overboard. Being very suspicious that it had been intentionally jettisoned, I stood eyeballing the perpetrator. I certainly didn't anticipate a confession, but in the ensuing half minute, yet another agitator piped up, "Oh Sarg, mine's gone too. Those brushes are slippery wee devils!"

I knew I was being had. "Okay, you two. Leave your buckets there and follow me." They knew that I knew, and they followed briskly. I took them at hell-raising pace, down stairs and along corridors, through hatchways, and finally slammed open the door of the Store's Quartermaster's Office.

Without preamble, I launched into my spiel. "These men seem to have developed Dropsy. They both lost paintbrushes over the side in the first ten minutes of the job." The elderly Warrant Officer put down his paperback, got slowly off his chair, and consoled me gently. "That seems to happen a lot. Maybe it's these lads not being used to the roll of the ship." I turned aside and rolled my eyes. The Med, that day, was as calm as a mill pond.

The Highlanders were as taken in by this as I was. Smiles appeared on their faces as if here was validation of their story. Before I could embark on a repudiation of his remarks, the sage conjured up two new paintbrushes, gave them to the almost giggling offenders.

"Now just a minute boys," he cautioned, taking all of us by surprise. As if anticipating this dilemma, he had at the ready two lengths of binder twine. With speed that I'd never have expected from one with such a rotund physique, he tied the brushes to each reluctant man's wrist, affixing them tighter than a tourniquet. "That should fix that problem," he said as he resumed his chair and his novel. Wordlessly we returned to the awaiting paint cans. As if by telepathy, the word got around. We never lost another brush all the way to Singapore. Needless to say the painting went on.

As we made our slow passage through the Suez Canal the heat was stifling. There isn't room for large ships to pass in the one hundred mile length of the actual canal. Halfway south in the Bitter Lakes, in an extensive widening of the natural waterway, south bound ships lay-up for four hours to allow the north bound convoy to pass.

It was the ideal place to have a full boat drill. The hospital permanent staff was involved in this, as it pertained to potentially dealing with injured personnel. When the call went out for volunteers to man the oars in the lifeboats, I grasped the opportunity for revenge of my own. My ten Highlanders looked great in the boat. None of them had ever seen an oar in their life, so it took an inordinate amount of time and sweat for them to row that lifeboat once round the one hundred yard-long Oxfordshire in that blistering heat. I watched, from the freshly painted railing, with a feeling of great satisfaction.

The next event in our back-and-forth one-upmanship drama happened in the Red Sea. A bucket of white paint went overboard. I saw the elbow that manufactured that 'accident' and hauled the offending owner down to the bowels of the ship at the double. I was sure the Quartermaster had experienced similar incidents in the past.

"Guess what?" I started. The old gent knew the answer before I had a chance to elaborate. "Ship rolls, bucket falls. Follow me." With my now anxious Glasgow lad in tow, we picked up a new bucket and brush and followed the old guy forward to the very front of the ship, still thirty feet below sea level.

The Quartermaster swung open a heavy wooden door of what was one of the ship's prison cells. The room was 6'x 6' x 10'in dimension. It had a 2"x 6" slot at eye level, the only aperture to the outside world. A shelf at knee height was the sole furnishing. He turned to my protégé whose suntan was disappearing by the second. "Paint it laddie, ceiling, walls, door and floor. I'll be back tomorrow." He slammed the door. It gets quite slippery on a painted floor, so by the time our pal was released next day, he was an albino.

Our ongoing 'cruise' called in at another couple of pink places. At Aden, a bustling oil fill-up stopover, we again had a four-hour shore leave. It was another intriguing spot for a thousand soldiers to stretch their legs and sample the local wares and beverages. Time aboard had taken its toll. A combination of forty-five degree Centigrade temperature, and temporary escape from supervision, created the perfect storm for over indulgence. By sheer happenstance, amongst the half dozen inebriated revelers fetched in by the Red Caps moments before we sailed, were two of my scoundrels. They spent seven days ensconced in the comforts of that three hundred-sixty cubic foot, recently painted, cell.

They'd chosen a most inopportune time to sample those accommodations at the furthermost forward part of the ship. Leaving Aden and venturing into the Indian Ocean, the ship encountered colossal seas. The prow was rising and falling thirty feet in the waves.

A few brave souls were on the top deck doing their best to emulate the future young Leonardo DiCaprio on the Titanic's bow, although I can't recall there being any available female beauty to play the part of Kate Winslet, the heroine. I imagine those incarcerated for their brief dalliance in Aden, felt that they too were on their way to Davey Jones' Locker.

The next pink stopover was in Colombo, Ceylon. As with many of the former British colonies, the name has changed. Today it is known as Sri Jayawadenapura-Kotte, Sri Lanka. Sadly, I recall little of the congested port on our four-hour touch on solid ground. It seemed a swarming mass, a comparable forerunner of today's 'Slumdog Millionaire' movie scenes. I'll offer it the benefit of the doubt, and assume that today it has improved in aesthetic status, and accordingly, as a tourist venue.

Familiarity with life aboard ship made the remaining seven days of the voyage to our destination, in Singapore, seem routine. There was the start of anticipation for what lay ahead, but we'd grown accustomed to our temporary home on the ship. By then, I'd become an old hand at maneuvering around the passages and stairwells, and I'd managed a workable truce with my gang. A third of the troops had been dropped off to their new posting in Aden, and another squad of signalmen in Ceylon. That meant less crowded accommodations, however, I never did spend any time on my allotted Bunk 146, merely visiting one last time to retrieve my possessions in readiness for disembarkation in Singapore.

The Oxfordshire plied back and forward from the UK to the Orient for another two years before being decommissioned as a troop ship in 1963. By that time, British Military personnel were being transported by air to various overseas postings. The Oxfordshire returned to Southampton carrying on its final voyage, ironically, a company of Royal Highland Fusiliers from their closing base in Malta. (No doubt the painting of every inch of railing continued en route.) The great ship was recommissioned as a cruise ship in Southampton and made its way back through the Suez to Australia to be the flag ship of the Sitmar Line, an Italian-owned venture that operated out of Sydney on the South Pacific passenger cruise circuit.

The newly renovated accommodations, offering first, second and third class cabins for a capacity of five hundred paying passengers were, presumably, more posh than the cramped accommodations of my time aboard. During its years as a cruise ship, the Oxfordshire was known as the 'Fun Ship'. In 1997, after forty years of faithful service, the old girl went to the wreckers in India, which by then was no longer pink on the map. No recognition was given to the great work performed by my painting crew of Highlanders so many years before.

> When I'm at the helm
> The world's my realm
> And I do it stylishly
> Port out Starboard home,
> Posh with a capital 'P'.

Early Days - Kinrara

Bless 'em all, bless 'em all
The long and the short and the tall
Bless all the sergeants and W.O. Ones
Bless all the corp'rals and their blinking sons
For we're saying good-bye to them all
As back to their billets they crawl
You'll get no promotion this side of the ocean
So cheer up my lads Bless 'em all
By Hughes/Lake

*T*he journey from Singapore to Kuala Lumpur by train took ten hours in 1961. That overnight, two hundred-fifty mile adventure was an eye-opener, as two hundred military personnel shared cramped quarters with a similar number of multinational civilian families.

'Fresh off the boat', quickly lost its meaning as combined factors of overcrowding, tropical heat, and the new exposure to Asian culture and customs, created an unforgettable experience. Sleeping accommodations on the train were supposedly single occupant upper and lower berths, but each was crammed with at least two soldiers and their masses of kit. Other, even more congested spaces housed whole families of the local population with adults and crying children squeezed into upper bunks between suitcases and assorted luggage. A bedraggled, flimsy curtain gave some hint of privacy, but did little to contain new, alien, aromas of midnight feeds of curry and other Asian delicacies. The troops too contributed their distinctive smells. We had had a festering hot day at the dispersal camp in Singapore before being shuffled aboard the train. En route, many of the eagle-eyed Brits had located a source of Tiger beer, the local brew, and had stocked up on enough for a seven day trip.

Two mildly inebriated soldiers, who'd obviously had a head start on the booze, informed me that this was their second, three-year tour in Malaya. I should have known better than to ask them, "What's it like?" They assured me that the train journey we were on was much better than their first trip north, six years earlier. That had been at the height of the 'emergency', the fourteen-year guerrilla warfare period of Malaya's history that had only recently been resolved. As we steamed our way north through the impenetrable jungle, they told stories of the days when there had been machine-gunners posted on top of the carriages, and of mass evacuations in the pitch black when the trains were ambushed. It was before the days of Google validation or repudiation, but I was left with an uneasy feeling of concern, to add to the physical discomforts of the trip. It took a long time to arrive at our destination.

Finally, with the sun starting to heat things up even more, we spilled out onto the already crowded platform in Kuala Lumpur, the capital city of Malaya. K.L. had started as a small settlement at the junction of two muddy rivers in the 1800's, when Chinese entrepreneurs pursued the much valued tin deposits in the area. Later, British pioneers with their eyes on the country's potential commercial value, helped settle the local squabbles in the area, and put yet one more pink spot on Queen Victoria's map of the Empire.

Kuala Lumpur's railway station was built of massive sandstone and tile to minimize the risk of fire that had gutted the city years earlier. The architecture was reminiscent of the great Indian Peninsular Railway Terminus in Bombay. That edifice had been described as, 'British Raj at its most vulgar, and splendid.' To me, getting wearily off that train, the station was a magnificent sight, huge arches and a mixture of colonial, oriental and Moorish design.

Eventually, I was ushered out through the massive pillared entry, and dragged my kit into a three-ton truck. I was the only passenger so I sat up front with the Malay Service Corps driver. He took great delight in terrifying me as he bulldozed his way through trishaws, scooters and taxis in the early morning traffic. Only much later I would realise that that had been a quiet Sunday morning in Kuala Lumpur.

As we merged into the suburbs and weaved our way along the Ampang River bank, the city quite suddenly ended and we entered unrelenting jungle and rubber plantations. The driver chatted away telling me how wonderful life was at the British Military Hospital Kinrara, just ten miles out of the city. The B.M.H. was to be my home and stomping ground for the next two joyous years. My driver had been absolutely spot-on in his description.

The grounds had been wrestled out of the surrounding jungle to accommodate a two hundred-bed hospital, along with living quarters for one hundred military personnel. Cognisant of the needs of the predominantly eighteen to twenty-five year old staff, a huge expanse of playing field had been cleared just outside of the main gates for such British pursuits as cricket, field hockey, rugby and soccer. Within the fenced compound, numerous tennis, badminton and volleyball courts ensured that recreation was an important element of life on that distant edge of the Empire.

With a cursory nod to the guard at the gate, my escort swept me right up to the Sergeants' Mess. I stumbled out of the vehicle, collected my kit, and watched him roar off down the road. I stood for a minute taking in the silence and beauty of the spot. There was a scent of flowers that turned out to be from a hedgerow of orchids. Green manicured lawns spread out around the buildings whose terraces and walkways were shaded by groves of banana fronds and lush tropical foliage.

Shortly, I was welcomed by Mutiah, the mess steward. The other staff members came out and were introduced. The cook, the water boy, the amah (the laundry lady), the gardener all welcomed me, but there was not a white face in sight. A bit surprised by the absence of my expected military cohorts, I asked where everybody was hiding.

"Oh, big party till 4 am," they explained, beaming to imply that it had been fun. I got tucked into a hearty breakfast and soon my fellow residents started to appear, no doubt disturbed from their slumbers by the departing truck. Midst welcomes and introductions, they advised, "Don't' eat too much. We've got Tiffin's at 11:00." My puzzlement must have shown. They explained that Sunday Brunch was scheduled, where everybody arrived for the regular get-together of the entire Sergeants' Mess members and their families. What a way to start my new life!

I was shown to my quarters, a pleasant airy room that I shared with a Gurkha, Sergeant Nabir Paul Rai, whose job was interpreter for the many Nepalese soldier patients in the hospital. It was the start of a great friendship, and part of my enduring high regard for the dynamic fearless soldiers who were so well respected for their immense contribution to the British and Commonwealth military services.

By two o'clock, curry lunch and a few welcoming beers, combined with a sleepless night on the train, caused me to crash for a much needed siesta. At five I was awakened and ushered down to the playing fields to watch the unit team in a rugby match. I cannot recall seeing much of the game that day as I was absorbed in the mainly female spectator crowd, cheering for the teams that were on the field. It was the ultimate boy meets girls, a very pleasant introduction to my new country. The post game socialising and celebration went on till midnight.

I should have been a bit more diligent in getting organised for the work-week ahead. Early next morning, somewhat hung-over, I got dressed for my scheduled meeting with the Commanding Officer. At breakfast, seeing my fellow sergeants dressed immaculately in newly-starched, tailored uniforms, I realised that my best 'fresh' outfit, that been retrieved from the bottom of my kit bag, wasn't up to scratch. Nobody made any comment about my wrinkled, ill-fitting uniform, so I proceeded down to the C.O.'s office. The journey was only two hundred yards but by the time I arrived, the already scorching sun and high level of anxiety, had me dripping with sweat. Not the most positive way to show up in front of my new boss.

He'd obviously seen similar first-day dishevelment. He just laughed and shook his head. "Saville Rows' sartorial elegance is slipping these days, I notice. Never mind, the amah will fix all that up and make you look human. Welcome to Kinrara." I'd anticipated a severe reprimand. I was liking what I saw and heard here. The orderly Sergeant got me into a dazzling white, starched coat to cover up my scruffy uniform, and we did a tour of the hospital.

On the first ward we visited, one of the young nurses I'd met at the rugby pitch blocked our path. At our meeting the previous day, I'd been wearing just a pair of shorts and sandals, proudly showing off my twenty-four day 'cruise' super bronze tan. "Oh you look different in clothes," she said loudly. I tried to laugh it off, but blushed like a nine year old. The whole ward was in hysterics. Seeing my discomfort, she whispered, "We'll cool you down with a beer tonight." Life has its up and downs.

The hospital had a hundred yard-long central covered walkway, with all the wards and departments set off at right angles in regimental layout. All the buildings were one-storey with over hanging roof extensions to provide shade. Most had wooden-shuttered windows that were thrown open at first light to allow free air passage throughout. Inside there were large, slow-turning ceiling fans to give some relief from the ninety degree Fahrenheit midday temperatures.

At both sides of the main corridor were two-foot wide, three-foot deep, monsoon drains to cope with the deluge of tropical storm rain that could, at times, amount to two inches in one hour. The drains occasionally filled to overflow levels, and at some stage almost everyone came to grief by falling into these chasms. Within my first week, I misjudged the width of one sharp concrete edge and in I went.

It wasn't long till I was into the full swing of life seven thousand miles from bonnie Scotland. Long before the era of Facebook and other instant communication magic, those miles were bridged by regular mail, especially from my mother. Years later, after my mother's death, I found the carefully filed letters that held my weekly account of my adventures. Those writings told tales of fun and youthful exuberance, intermingled with gratifying success at work, and occasionally, times of anguish and failure.

The camaraderie of those isolated overseas postings, especially so in military hospitals, was a feature that still brings back fond memories half a century later. The good times of those days surface easily to brighten my days, while the times of hurt have gently faded. Leg-pulling was rife. Each of us endured it, later to laugh at the experience. An early such incident for me came at one seven o'clock morning roll call parade. The myriad of common and incomprehensible names showed the spectrum of nationalities serving in that Commonwealth army hospital. Unexpectedly one morning, the Company Sergeant Major called out, "Sgt. Farish, call the roll."

I started out reasonably confidently, with the first few names on the list of the sixty personnel in attendance, in alphabetical order, "Anderson, Brown, Coombes..."

Interrupting me, the C.S.M. bellowed from the back of the parade, "Louder Sgt., I can't hear you!" Becoming quite flustered, I felt the paper shaking in my hand as I tried to decipher the next names: "Danbahadur Gurung, Dhalbasi Rai, Dillongbasi Sing." I stuttered like a six year old in front of his Grade One class. It was a complete disaster. Momentarily I looked up and saw that every face had a smile, and some men were silently rocking in laughter.

The voice from the back shouted, "Corporal Mohamed Rai, rescue that poor Sgt." Only then did I realise I'd been the brunt of a frequently repeated joke, played on the most recent arrival in camp. The young Malay rattled off the rest of the roll call list of Malay, Chinese, Indian, Gurkha, Brit, Aussie and Kiwi names as if he'd practiced all night for the task. I did gain a tiny bit of solace when he struggled with McFarquharson. Back in the mess for breakfast, with much back slapping and frivolity, the C.S.M came as close as that rank ever got to apologizing, by saying he'd buy me a beer that night.

Gradually, after hearing stories of the other bygone similar catastrophes, including episodes of tears and rage, things settled down. I never did admit how close I'd come to a similar reaction. As I became a real, 'old soldier', it was my delight, a few months later, to shout from the back of the parade, "Louder Sgt., I cannot hear you," to the quaking newest, 'Whitey from Blighty'.

Although the morning parade was one of the many mildly irksome necessities of military life, it was a feature that got all workers ready for their daily tasks in punctual fashion. Years later, I'd roll my eyes in exasperation when some of the young physiotherapists in my clinic would scamper in to work, predictably a few minutes late, to again apologize profusely to their watch-checking patients. I'd think back fondly to bygone times at B.M.H. Kinrara, and the non-negotiable punctuality demanded in those, 'early days'.

Multi-tasking

*L*ong before the word came into vogue, in modern-day vocabulary, 'multi-tasking' was an apt description of my life as a young sergeant in Malaya. I now tire just thinking of the variety of projects that landed on my shoulders there, half a century ago.

The R.A.M.C. in Kuala Lumpur still had a significant number of the last of the National Service conscripts serving out their mandatory two years. Amongst the dozen or so who lived in residence in the sergeants' quarters, were a fabulous group of qualified pharmacists, laboratory technicians, radiographers and teachers. All were in their early twenties, having deferred enlistment till they had completed university or college graduation. In addition, our unit was the envy of all the other British, Australian and New Zealand land forces, for one, simple, obvious reason: There were fifty nurses living in our unit, officers and other ranks of the Queen Alexandra's Royal Army Nursing Corps (Q.A.R.A.N.C.). Life was good, and it almost seemed that sports and socializing were occasionally interrupted with actual work and military duties. Those duties, however, proved to be extremely varied. A case in point was when the Commanding Officer called me in to his office within days of my arrival.

"Sgt. Farish, beyond your physiotherapy duties we'll expect you to be involved in other activities in the unit, in your spare time. I've got just the job for you to begin with. I want you to carry out the Annual Physical Fitness test on all members under thirty-five years of age. It's a straight forward sort of thing. It's right up your street. My chief clerk will fill you in on the details. Dismissed."

I stumbled out of his office after the obligatory salute and about turn. The young chief clerk was smirking, well aware that I hadn't had the opportunity to say a single word during the C.O.'s monologue.

"Piece of cake," the clerk assured me, implying that the job I'd been handed was routine. "Straight forward," he repeated the C.O.'s words. "It's the once per year physical performance test." He casually flipped the instruction sheet my way along with a list of the names of the unit personnel.

"Just do ten each day after work and you'll be finished in a couple of weeks." As if as an afterthought he added, "They haven't done it for three or four years and I don't think they'll like it." He actually giggled.

"I thought it was an annual P.E. test!"

"It's supposed to be, but the C.O.'s new and so are you. No, they definitely won't like it."

Storming off with the instruction sheet in hand, it didn't take me long to realise that the assignment was going to be annoying rather than difficult. I set about organising a schedule for the first lucky group. The test seemed ludicrously easy: (1) jump across an eight foot ditch; (2) carry a man of your own weight one hundred yards; (3) run one mile in twelve minutes; (4) climb a rope; (5) march five miles.

It was still ninety degrees Fahrenheit when my first group assembled, unenthusiastically, next afternoon on the edge of the football field. A healthy man could have almost stepped across the eight feet between the two markers laid out on the grass, but in his endeavour, one lout managed to sprain an ankle. The man-carrying task became complicated when there was no-one to match up with the barely five foot tall, ninety pound Malay orderly. Nor would anyone even try to carry the two hundred-forty pound cook. There was no rope available, so that exercise was voided, and calamity struck when the same overweight cook collapsed a quarter mile into the run. He was carried off to the Emergency Department where he made a suspiciously rapid, full recovery. I called off the project.

Next morning, expecting a reprimand, I was delighted to receive a phone call from the chief clerk to tell me the whole program had been shelved. Influential in that decision was the fact that the cook, who'd done the near-death act, was the Officers' Mess chef.

Just weeks before my arrival in Malaya, the country had had a disastrous landslide at the village of Ringlet in the Cameron Highlands. Caused by a three-day monsoon deluge, a massive section of hillside slammed into the community, wiping out the frail housing, killing twenty residents, and injuring many others. Commonwealth troops from close by had joined in the search and rescue for survivors. A spin-off from that tragic event affected me early in my stay and became one more learning experience.

Soon after my short lived P.E. test debacle, I was again hauled in to the C.O.'s office, where he outlined a new edict that had come from the powers that be, higher up.

He started off with, "Do you know anything about tents Sergeant?" I should have been on guard, suspicious, or at least smart enough to smell a trap. In my naivety, and anxious to recoup some semblance of credibility following the fitness fiasco, I foolishly enlarged on my miniscule knowledge of tents. I chatted about my years of Scout camping, and the tent we had put up in the back garden as a boy. As I described that four person shelter, embellished to sound like a twenty-capacity marquee, I dug a hole for myself that I'd soon regret.

He cut me off, mid-soliloquy, "Good, you're in charge of the new Mass Casualty Tenting Project. See the chief clerk for details."

The ever-shadowing clerical assistant rolled his eyes and, with difficulty, avoided breaking into laughter. "You'll regret that boastful outburst," he said, and he was right again.

Three days later, at the appointed four pm, my team of ten men, all non-volunteers, rendezvoused beside a three ton truck stacked with poles, ropes and enough canvas to cover the entire blistering-hot football field. Based on information learned during the Ringlet avalanche, the authorities had decided we should practice setting up a tent hospital in the off-chance one should be needed in an emergency.

One solitary older lad acknowledged he'd been attached to a field ambulance company years before, but had never been involved in assembling a tent. None of the others had even seen one. It took us more than half an hour to unload the contents of the truck, coincidentally finishing at the exact arrival time of the C.O., who had expected to see the 60'x20' tent already erected.

"I'm told ten men can put up these tents in forty minutes," he said, looking at his watch.

At seven o'clock, darkness stopped play, with the sagging main outline of the structure looking its ugliest. It was uplifting for the entire hospital staff's morale, as every member found time to wander down to the front gates next morning to laugh at the unfinished exhibit.

Again at four pm next day, we re-attacked and finally got things ship-shape before dark. The C.O. was not impressed by our performance and ordered us to practice raising and dismantling the #$:%* tent from dawn to dusk on that following Saturday and Sunday. It was great for the tan, but devastating for the psyche.

It was further ordained that from then on, that crew would instantly respond to the signal of three, ten-second blasts on the fire siren, and immediately begin to assemble the tent hospital. Two days later, just as I was uncapping my first after-work beer, the darn hooter sounded. The boss stood there, stop-watch in hand, less than impressed with our two hour and three minute effort. Practices went on once a week for a few weeks. We never did break the two hour record. Then as all great ideas do, this one faded into oblivion.

Word must have gotten around that I was the new kid on the block who'd be ripe for taking on chores that no one else wanted to do. The Chief Medical Physician talked me into doing cardiographs. It wasn't exactly rocket science, and he took all of three minutes to instruct me, but thereafter, I'd be called once a week or so to do this nuisance job. Of course I hadn't a clue about how to read them, but unloading that 'special task' from my job description proved difficult.

Taking my turn every ten days or so on overnight duty as Orderly Sergeant was another learning experience that brought lots of surprises. One part of this work was the prompt 9:30 pm closing of the canteen. The Naafi was the only source of booze for the men and junior nurses, and was a decidedly popular establishment. From time to time, things got a bit out of hand due to overindulgence in the really cheap beer. Outside military personnel, visiting their buddies on the wards, had a habit of slugging back a few pints before they returned to their units.

One memorable, face-to-face incident, resolved surprisingly peacefully. A group of Australians, renowned for their insatiable thirst, and subsequent flashpoint spirited reactions, had ordered yet another round of pints right at the barman's last call. Trying to negotiate a quiet exit, I convinced them to do a race to down these final jugs. Three hulking lads, all well over six feet tall complied, finishing off their suds in record time. But a chirpy little pal, surely the smallest Aussie I'd ever seen, took umbrage at my scheme and started mouthing off at me. I envisioned real trouble ahead and my nervousness must have been evident. The biggest of the group smiled, and said, "Relax Sarg, we'll take him home." He tucked the squirming noisy one under his colossal arm and waved to me as they ambled off.

"Whew," I thought, "that could have been nasty."

I learned another approach one evening as I supervised the almost-empty emergency department while the on-duty medic went off on his midnight supper break. The only patient was a belligerent drunk who had quite a few bruises and lacerations resulting from a fight downtown. He wouldn't quieten down, and I was glad to see the thirty year old medic return, accompanied by a female nurse. Eying the cute young woman, the drunk went into overdrive with lecherous comments. The medic had heard enough. He seized the edge of the stretcher trolley and pulled it away from the wall. In a flash, he rolled the screeching drunk off the back and rammed the trolley into him two or three times. "Oh dear, help me Sergeant, he's fallen off the bed." We dragged the now silent offender back onto the bench. Three sober witnesses tried hard to avoid laughing. What a lesson I'd learned from that smart 'old soldier'.

On my next night shift I had a completely different experience. In the wee hours, a Malay driver brought in two stretchers bearing the charred bodies of two young soldiers, the result of a horrendous, fiery crash. The driver and I hauled them into the morgue, a tiny, isolated, concrete-block building hidden away at the perimeter fence. Nothing could make the driver stay a second longer, and he vanished into the pitch black night leaving me alone. I spent the next half-hour chopping up two blocks of ice into chunks to pack around the remains, to offset the effect of the tropical heat. I'd heard how peeved the pathologist became if he had to face, 'hot' corpses for his post-mortems. Oh how I wished for air-conditioning, and especially for the companionship of a living soul. Nothing from my prior experience and blasé confidence, instilled by bygone funeral humour in my Scottish family home, helped fend off the unsettling trauma of that night.

From time to time I was loaned out to another B.M.H. in Taiping, two hundred miles north. These temporary visits were delightful interludes and brought their own excitement, challenges and rewards. They also gave me the opportunity to have short weekend visits to almost-paradise island locations off the northwest coast. Oh, the army could be a rough assignment at times!

Christmas was a time of very mixed emotions around the hospital. Other than mail, there was no way to contact families back in UK, as phone communication wasn't available for the rank and file of service personnel. Consequently, the feeling of isolation was intense, and great effort was made to get everyone through the strained atmosphere of seeing Santa in the tropics. There were concerts, dances, lavish feasts, and special efforts made in caring for each other. Compounding the aura of homesickness, returns to UK were accelerated just before Christmas for those nearing completion of their time overseas. This was a bonus for those leaving, allowing them to be home for the festive season, but it brought about highly emotional send offs at the Kuala Lumpur railway station. For many, this marked the end of relationships and long-term friendships.

One heart breaker occurred when friends of a departing nurse brought her yellow Labrador to the train. The beautiful animal had been her constant companion during her stay, although this flagrantly defied the rules. As the train pulled away from the station, the dog slipped its lead and raced after its faithful mistress for half a mile before the poor beast could be tethered.

On Christmas night the church service was packed, and afterwards there was an uncharacteristic tolerance for all-night festivities and partying. Then at three am I was called to the ward to treat an emergency patient. He was a Maori, a member of the nearby New Zealand Regiment at Malacca on the west coast. He had hit a rock on a dive into the sea and suffered a broken neck. At admission, he was a quadriplegic, with a tracheotomy opening in his windpipe to allow suction of phlegm and secretions that were building up in his lungs. As I joined the team working nonstop to keep him alive, a group of his soldier buddies arrived to give him support. They were part of a musical ensemble and set up their instruments beside his bed. They played and sang haunting Polynesian songs throughout the night. There wasn't a dry eye in the place as that beautiful sound spread through the suddenly silent hospital. A few days later, with no change in his condition, he was air lifted back to New Zealand for specialist care.

Amongst the diverse activities that unit personnel were involved in, one was particularly rewarding and memorable. A gang of twenty or so of us crammed into a three ton truck, complete with soccer balls, badminton equipment and a supply of soft drinks. Our destination was a leper colony only twenty miles from the hospital, tucked away on a narrow, little-used road leading into the secret depths of the jungle. Our visit was at the invitation of a social worker from that hidden 'kampong' or village. We had been assured that none of the residents there would pose any health risk to us. The majority of the villagers were undergoing prolonged medical treatment, some for the rest of their lives, but only a few showed much sign of the disease.

Leprosy affects the nerves and other tissues. It is spread by human contact and droplet transmission through saliva, and is most prevalent in areas of poverty and unhygienic living conditions. Known and described since Biblical times, the disfigurement, muscle wasting, and deformity from leprosy leads to fear and social stigma that forced suffers to be ostracized and banished to remote locations even today.

Our visit brought obvious joy to the residents. Even in the 1960's many had severe psychological suffering because they had been rejected by their families living nearby. The young army group were soon mingling, playing sports, singing and sharing laughter with the surprised, reclusive people. I like to think that our community venture was also an equally positive experience for the young 'foreign' service personnel in the truck as well.

Near the end of my time at B.M.H. Kinrara, I was reminded of one of my earlier tasks there. It was six months after the last Mass Casualty Tenting Project practice when to my surprise, the almost-forgotten three blasts were heard necessitating the setting up of the mini-hospital. The stop-watch man was there again, this time, to my hardly concealed delight, almost foaming at the mouth when he realized that five of my team had been posted back to the UK. A new team was recruited the next day, and immediately confirmed their ineptitude by taking over three hours to assemble the tent. That led to a few more dreary practices that did nothing to speed things up. Eventually the futility of the program led to its discontinuation.

By that time I had been posted upcountry for my final year of that overseas stay. It was time to move on. All my young National Service pals had gone home. With their departure, the exuberance and frivolity of youth that had brought irreplaceable camaraderie, faded away.

I was ready for new horizons, challenges, and opportunities for multi-tasking at my next posting, near the top of the backbone of Malaya, in the six thousand foot high Cameron Highlands.

An Officer and A Gentleman

Serving as a twenty-three year old physiotherapist sergeant in the British Military Hospital at Kinrara was as enjoyable as life can get in the army. The work was interesting and rewarding, and didn't interfere too much with my major priorities of rugby in the monsoon season and football and cricket in the dry times. Tennis and badminton were also fitted in, and there was a bit of 'cherchez la femme'.

There was a great camaraderie amongst all the hospital staff, who were mainly in the nineteen to thirty age range, although the matron, some senior administrators and the chief surgeon were a bit ancient, reaching almost into their forties.

Occasionally this comfortable status was rudely interrupted. One of those memorable moments was my unexpected meeting with a General. I was ill-at-ease with the prospect of hobnobbing with the gentry far above my social class as a meagre young non-commissioned officer in the R.A.M.C.

I had a few minutes to wonder about the meeting as I wheeled my short-wave diathermy machine into the officers' ward. I was about to meet Sir Cedric Simpson.* Knighted for his outstanding contribution to his country in various wars and skirmishes throughout the world in his previous almost half century of military life, he had been seconded after retirement from the British Army, and was on loan to advise the Malayan government. He was indisputably, at sixty-five years young, 'The Boss', to whom all Army, Navy and Air Force commanders were answerable.

The affliction that merited my medical ministrations was massive bruising, pain and loss of movement in his hip, buttock, and upper thigh. The injury was a result of the General having parted ways from his horse, at the gallop, during a gentlemanly game of polo. He hadn't fallen off the animal, he had been thrown! Adding insult to injury, it had happened on the Padang, the lush manicured sports field in front of the Selangor Cricket Club, with Royalty observing the incident.

I could sense the tension as I passed through the open section of the ward that housed a few junior officers. Normally these young men were full of laughter and fun, but as the head nurse escorted me through, there was an ominous silence about the place.

At the far end of the ward, a young Lieutenant in full dress uniform stood rigidly in front of the closed doors of the special air-conditioned suite that housed the General. The lad was trying unsuccessfully to balance strict officialdom with a touch a mild nonchalance. His location and stance made it clear his job was to keep out all but the invited. He eyed me up and down, glared suspiciously at my machine, and commanded me to wait. He swivelled, almost saluted his reflection in the window, and tapped delicately on the door he had been guarding. The door opened a few inches and a face appeared. With a deferential whisper the Lieutenant passed on the message to the Major inside. Another peremptory, "Wait!" came from within. I could hear the message being passed up the line, somewhat apologetically.

An upper-class authoritative voice exclaimed, "Excellent, bring him in." I almost heard the crowd roar "Break a leg!" as I ventured onto centre stage.

Before I could move, the door opened. There was a furtive gathering up of papers and charts as the General addressed the unseen group within that enclave. "It shouldn't take very long, just pop into Matron's office and I'm sure she'll fix you up with a cup of tea. I'll get Major Wilson* to call you as soon as I'm available."

I was awestruck as top ranking officers of air, sea and land forces emerged from the room. They sallied forth with brusque authority, clearly annoyed that I'd interrupted their high-level conference. I squeezed past Lt. Jones,* now at rigid attention at the door, and took in the amazing site of the patient in his silk dressing gown and striped pyjamas. He had a great mop of silver wavy hair capping his bronzed, friendly and weathered face.

In seconds, he had made a full assessment of the terrified youngster in front of him. "I'm Sergeant Farish, Sir Cedric, Sir," I stuttered then fell silent, stunned. There was a click as the door closed and the Major was back on-guard inside the room.

"That will be just fine Major, why don't you pop along and make sure that the Commanders are being well looked after. I'm sure young Jones can hold the fort out there."

The Major left and I set up for the treatment with expediency, yet great care to ensure every possible safety measure and precaution. I gave the General an embellished version of expected results of this wonder machine, and reassured him that he'd feel no pain and that I'd be out of there in fifteen minutes.

We got into conversation after he had expressed gratitude for my fitting his treatment into my busy schedule. I'm sure the General was aware that the entire functioning of the hospital was stopped to ensure his needs were instantly met. I tried to console him that things might have been much worse. "You could have been killed Sir, falling off that horse."

"At the time, I almost wished I had been," he pouted. "Damned embarrassing right there of all places."

He settled back and murmured appreciation as the heat soothed his pain. "Where's your home in Scotland, Sergeant?" Ah hah, my dialect had shown through during my professional explanations.

"I'm from Dumfries, Sir," I answered.

"Really!" he exclaimed, showing sincere interest. "I'm quite familiar with Dumfries; I used to visit out near Holywood for pheasant shooting, and grouse, and a bit of salmon fishing, of course. Lovely estate, they hosted me so well." He was referring to one of the great ancestral homes discretely enveloped in wrought iron railings and rhododendrons not far from my home.

I couldn't resist a bit of name dropping. "That would be with Sir Francis Johnson*, Sir, wouldn't it?"

His eyes nearly popped out of his head at my question. "Why yes, do you know him?" he asked with incredulity in his voice.

The devil in me drove me on. "Oh yes, very well, Sir. I was often in that great household, lovely people."

"Really?" He was still suspicious that I could possibly be regularly associating with one of his knighted peers.

I couldn't hold back the giggle as I explained. "I was Sir Francis' postman and took the mail right up into his kitchen every day."

The General exploded in the loudest roar of laughter. He realised I'd gently pulled his leg, so to speak. He lay there and guffawed as only an English aristocrat would do.

The young Lieutenant burst the door open, alarmed at the sounds, and stood wide-eyed. "Are you alright Sir?" he asked.

"Yes, yes I'm fine, having a great time actually." The young guard retreated quite baffled.

The timer on the machine sounded the end of the treatment and I took a hasty retreat, lest I overstay my welcome. As I left, the great man reassured me he already felt much better, and he was looking forward to my next visit. The Lieutenant gave me the strangest look as I pushed my machine down the corridor.

The General responded well to my treatments, and we developed a totally unexpected connection as senior officer and therapist that did not resemble my initial humble anticipation, due to the immense difference in our ranks.

My admiration for Sir Cedric heightened even more following an incident when he was attending for further treatments as an outpatient. I'd applied a tensor bandage to control the swelling high up on the thigh and was a bit anxious that the bandage might slacken off as he went about his travels. Even before he reached his Rolls Royce at the front of the hospital, I spied him bent over, gathering up the end of the errant bandage and tucking it into his stocking.

I was on the edge of utter collapse as the phone rang and the Commanding Officer's outraged voice came over the line. His office was right at the front of the hospital, close to where the General had been doing his running-repairs on the bandage. I was sure the C.O. must have seen the disaster. "Don't you ever let the General come here for treatment without forewarning me of his scheduled visit!" he screamed, and slammed down the phone. That was an unexpected reprieve.

Two days later the General returned for another treatment. I'd informed the C.O.'s office, and of course the Colonel was there strutting about in welcome. To make matters worse he escorted Sir Cedric right to the door of the physiotherapy department. I sighed with relief as he said, not really meaning it, "I'll leave you in Sgt. Farish's capable hands," and bade the General farewell.

I'd sweated for two whole days about how to address the problem of the bandage foul-up. I was sure the great man was well aware that I knew what had happened. Cautiously, not daring to look him in the eye, I admitted I had worried about how secure the bandage had been. Quietly he acknowledged that it had, "loosened up a bit," but he was quite sure it had still been of some benefit.

After he left I almost collapsed in gratitude and relief. I still fondly remember the General as a truly exceptional person who understood how to combine humility with great power. I hold him in great admiration as one deserving of my lifelong description as an 'Officer and a Gentleman'.

The Great Gurkhas

*D*uring part of the British Empire's building era of the 1830's, the East India Trading Company suffered heavy casualties in their incursion into what would subsequently become Nepal. Prudence overcame valor, so they signed a hasty treaty with their foes permitting the recruitment of soldiers from their former enemies. From that propitious beginning, Britain obtained an important addition to its fighting forces. The tiny men from that high Himalayan area surrounding Gorkha, were the early ancestors of the Gurkha regiments of today.

Over the past two centuries, generations of these fearless hill warriors have competed to enlist in the Army. Two-hundred thousand fought in the two world wars and forty-three thousand died in that service of the British Monarchy. The Gurkhas have been in every theatre of war and skirmish around the world. They fought at Gallipoli, Mesopotamia, Africa, Italy, Normandy, Burma, Malaya, Cyprus, Northern Ireland, the Falklands, and now in Afghanistan. They've been everywhere!

Described using every superlative including 'indomitable', 'uncomplaining', and 'unwavering', they are the bravest of the brave. In military terms, they offer a combination of qualities that make the ideal soldier: Tough, durable, loyal, amenable to discipline, and brave. The Victoria Cross, the highest recognition for valour in the British Services, has been awarded to thirteen Gurkha members of the British military, attesting to this fact.

During a three-day visit to Stoke Mandeville early in my physiotherapy training, I met my first Gurkha, at that world-renowned centre for rehabilitation of severe spinal injury. He was the tiny, brown-skinned man with an indefatigable spirit and the irrepressible smile that shone like a beacon amongst the assembled wheel-chair-bound paraplegics.

I had not looked forward to that required visit, as the prospect of meeting hundreds of permanently paralyzed individuals didn't gel with my vision of an exciting career of caring for fit, sports-oriented athletes. Twenty year old Nabir Gurong Singh, and the enthusiasm of the hand-picked staff at that centre, changed my perspective forever.

Nabir had been critically injured in a training accident in Northern Malaya, fracturing his lower spine and causing lifelong paralysis of his legs. He had never been to the UK before this tragedy but, as a British serviceman, he had been flown to London to receive what was considered to be the best available rehabilitation in the world.

In his wheelchair, drenched in sweat from his endeavours, he caught my eye the moment I saw him. His rudimentary grasp of English did not stop him from enthusiastically joining in the class led by a young physiotherapist. I was in awe of the spirit of that group. Indicative of the fame of the centre, there were patients from all over the world.

Although I wasn't aware of it from viewing him in his wheelchair, Nabir was just over five feet tall, quite typical of the height of Gurkha soldiers. His severely wasted legs, a mere shadow of their immensely muscled pre-injury size, were at odds with those of his sturdy fellow countrymen. A lifetime of walking up and downhill, to and from their homes high in the Himalayas, create the disproportionally large lower body of inhabitants of that mountainous region. Not surprisingly, many of those hill tribesmen carry the heavy loads of supplies to the base camps of Everest, and have the greatest number of ascents of that high point of the world.

That brief three-day encounter with Nabir was the prelude to my three-year interaction with Gurkha soldiers. Their main training base was in Malaya which was for most of those young men, their first travel of more than thirty miles from their home village. In Malaya the jungle with its almost sea level tropical heat and humidity was a drastic change from the rarified atmosphere and cool air of their home altitude.

On arrival at B.M.H. Kinrara, by sheer coincidence, another Nabir, Sgt. Nabir Paul Rai, a Gurkha interpreter, shared a room with me for a year, and we became good friends. I first arrived there early on a Sunday morning, and was amazed to see a group of patients playing volleyball on a bare patch of grass near one of the wards. I asked a new British colleague to explain what was happening. He was still bleary-eyed and struggling from a hangover from his Saturday night overindulgence.

"Oh those crazy buggers, I don't think they ever sleep. They are out there at the crack of dawn every day and they'd still be there till midnight if it didn't get dark. They are the Gurkhas," he summed up, as if that explained everything.

At a later date, joining them in a game, I was shocked to find that many of those five-footers could spike the ball over the ten foot high net. They were fanatically competitive in many sports and darted around like little demons on basketball and badminton courts. Football was yet another game that they played tirelessly and with skill. One of my strengths on the hospital football team was my ability, 'in the air', the art of heading the ball. At six feet tall I was convinced I'd have a distinct advantage with this skill when playing against the Gurkhas. Being frequently out-jumped by the wee men dispelled that myth.

A full ward in the hospital in Kinrara was set aside for the treatment of tuberculosis. The majority of the bedridden clientele were Gurkhas, perhaps indicative of their susceptibility to the vast difference in climate from their homeland, or possibly the crowded living conditions in the barracks. The prevalent treatment at that time, in addition to specific medicinal intervention, was complete bed rest for prolonged periods, sometimes six months to a year. The tolerance and patience of even those usually-disciplined young men wore down as days stretched into weeks and months. Several beds would be moved together to allow small groups of the sick to play cards together. As in every sphere of their existence, the Gurkhas played extremely competitively. Inevitably disputes occurred overriding their inherent mutual respect and team spirit.

Contrary to hospital standing orders, some of the Gurkhas had smuggled their coveted kukris into the ward. At the height of an altercation, one of the twelve-inch blades would be withdrawn from its scabbard and brandished. As discipline and civility was restored, the perpetrator still felt obliged to live out the traditional requirement of drawing blood with the weapon, before it could be replaced in its sheath.

The usual method of restoring honour in these circumstances was a discrete blood-letting skin scratch. On one occasion, however, the still-angry youth sliced deep into his wrist, severing tendons and suffering a serious wound. It took surgery and prolonged rehabilitation to restore his wrist to normal function. The soldier was admonished for disobeying hospital rules, but recognition of the long-standing traditions of regimental customs resulted in a penalty less than might otherwise have been given for a self-inflicted wound.

Treating these amazing men, I was always delighted with their compliance with exercise regimes I'd ask them to perform. The desire to get fit to return to their regiment was always their goal. Ensuring that they didn't overdo their programs was part of the unusual challenge I faced.

An unforgettable embarrassment in that particular area befell me in dealing with a patient recovering following surgery for a torn knee cartilage. He was progressing well and I had him doing step-ups to strengthen his thigh muscles. Just after he started, I got a phone call from the surgeon asking me to run up to the nearby ward to see an interesting x-ray. Anticipating the visit to be a thirty second venture, I told the patient to keep on doing the exercise. One thing led to another, possibly a dalliance with a nurse, and my stay in the ward stretched to fifteen minutes. Suddenly aware of my gross error, I bolted back to the physiotherapy department, wrenched the door open, and as could have been predicted, saw that the Gurkha was still going up and down on those two steps. The floor for six feet around him was awash in sweat, but there was a huge smile on his face. I implored him to sit down and rest. "Why didn't you sit down when you got tired?" I pleaded with him.

"You order me no stop Sergeant," he said. "I not tired."

I'm sure he would have continued till he collapsed if I hadn't returned. I was appalled by my unprofessional error and hastily got him onto a treatment bed and applied ice to his already swelling knee. A few hours later, the bloated joint was at bursting point, and I was terrified that the incision might split open. I expected to get a severe, well-deserved, reprimand from the surgeon. Instead, in the middle of that open ward with twenty other patients and staff observing, he roared with laughter when I explained what had transpired.

"You don't know much about Gurkhas, do you?" he said.

For a week I sweated it out while the resilient recipient of my mistake gradually improved, the smile never leaving his face. Perhaps he was laughing at me rather than with me. Fortunately, he made a complete recovery, and I learned an important lesson.

In today's malpractice-dominated world in North America, I'm sure I would have been sued for grievous dereliction of duty and professional standards. Of course, a similar event would be unlikely to happen here because nobody other than a Gurkha would continue to exercise unsupervised for that length of time. Nowadays I'd be told in non-ambiguous terms that I was a !xy!xx idiot, and rightly so.

The reputation of the famous Gurkha regiment as stealthy jungle fighters was almost folklore. To hear the deference and respect accorded to them by other Malay warfare participants told a story in itself. Tales of Gurkha skills and fearlessness relayed by Royal Marine Commandos, Special Air Service paratroopers, and hardened Aussie, Kiwi and British Infantrymen, none of those individuals exactly 'softies', solidified the deserved acclaim of the Nepalese.

An example of the widespread awareness of the fear they engendered happened in the Cameron Highlands. I was sitting in the hospital front gardens chatting with a couple of nurses when a wobbling intoxicated patient returned from an afternoon leave pass downtown. Spying the fair maidens, he made some lurid invitations. I recalled the old song lyrics entering my head, "What shall we do with the drunken sailor?" As if in answer to these words, two Gurkha patients walked past. I called out to them, "Take that man back to the ward!" They went into instant action and had the offending, much-larger man quickly hustled away.

"Get those animals off me!" I heard his plaintive cries as they frog-marched him out of sight. It was the easiest-problem solving I'd ever managed. I like to think my brilliant initiative was influential in the success of my afternoon's amorous pursuits.

Seeing the Gurkhas in their dress uniforms on parade was a sight to behold. The precision of their marching, their starched, tailored, green uniforms proudly showing the shoulder patches of crossed kukris, topped-off with their traditional wide-brimmed hats at the prescribed jaunty angle, even eclipsed the sight of a Scottish Kilted Regiment. Despite their obvious contribution to the British military, the Gurkhas were poorly treated by that same military. One example was a long-lasting agreement that their pay would be similar to Gurkhas enlisted in the Indian army. That rule meant that the amount of pay for Gurkhas was an abominable, fraction of the amount given to British servicemen of similar rank. Equally unfairly, although many Gurkhas and their families were stationed in the UK at Crookham, (my old medical corps-training base near Aldershot), they were required to return to Nepal when they retired from the army.

Protracted political petitions by civilian and military supporters, and belated acknowledgment of the immense contribution of the Gurkhas, has recently brought about the successful overturning of these appalling injustices. Gurkhas are now paid comparable rates to their British fellow soldiers, and can now receive appropriate pensions and settlement rights for themselves and their dependent families in the UK after retirement.

I offer my grateful thanks for many wonderful memories and the learning opportunities the Gurkhas gave to me. I shall never forget them, the bravest of the brave, the Great Gurkhas.

A Town Like Alice

*P*art of the rites of passage on an overseas military base was the individual handing down (or dumping) of goods and trappings accumulated in a three-year stay in that location by each serving member. British Military Hospital Kinrara, just ten miles outside the city limits of Kuala Lumpur, Malaya, had its share of those 'great sales' as departing 'Back to Blighty' boys and girls tried to offload excess baggage. Many of the items needing new owners were total junk, but occasionally a priceless gem surfaced.

Shortly after my arrival in 1961, I became the proud owner of a sixth or seventh hand-down of a distinguished antique car. It was a 1947 Rover 12, from an era when white-wall tires on spoke wheels were sheltered by huge flared mudguards. Fronted by a glistening chrome radiator grill and two enormous protruding twelve-inch diameter headlights, the six foot long engine-covering was home to the very conspicuous side mounted spare wheel.

The windshield could be folded down using a hand crank, and in combination with the slide-back roof vent, offered a full-blast of cooling air long before air-conditioning came into vogue. Discovered only during the first monsoon deluge, the closure mechanism of the vent was temperamental and caused severe dampening of the bliss of my first evening date.

The car was a beauty, steel grey in colour, although showing the results of years of demon sun rays and the customary wrinkles of age and hard wear inflicted on it by frequently inebriated British service personnel. However, at four hundred Malay dollars, (about one hundred Canadian) I had wheels.

In the back seat, thrown-in to make the deal more attractive, was a box of novels that the previous owner had failed to sell for cash. I selected a dozen or so before jettisoning the remainder on the wards where patients were always ready for such time-filling distractions.

One paperback in particular caught my eye. It was a dog-eared, much thumb-marked edition, with pages folded over where previous readers had documented their progress through its chapters. The cover picture, albeit stained with a beer bottle imprint, showed a slouch hat wearing Aussie outbacker and the inevitable beautiful young woman in his arms, whispering sweet nothings in the palm-treed tropical sunset. The back cover synopsis made the book a 'must read' for me: "Tells of a young woman who miraculously survived a Japanese death march in World War II, and an Australian soldier, also a prisoner of war, who offered to help her even at the cost of his own life."

The novel, *A Town Like Alice*, by Nevil Shute, although using locations in Malaya for the story background, told of an actual tragic sequence of events that occurred in Sumatra in 1942. There, a group of eighty European women and children, prisoners of the invading Japanese armies, were forced to march along jungle trails from camp to camp for twelve hundred miles over two and a half years. Only thirty people survived. I was hooked by that book, re-

reading it several times. I decided I would try to follow the travels the author described in Malaya, and eventually check out the Australian locations of the story.

Before starting on my first journey, I had begun to master the idiosyncrasies and caprices of my Rover. The tires were well worn and had a penchant for punctures so I became adept at wheel change, although getting the inner tube patched was problematic in some of the isolated villages. The locals could fix flats in bicycle tires but were woefully inexperienced in automobile repair, and not surprisingly, as there wasn't a single motorized vehicle in those out-of-the way places. I was amazed that in a country in which rubber production was one of the major natural resources, I couldn't find tires for that old car.

I did become proficient at addressing one of the R 12's frequent hiccups of carburetor malfunction. The remedy was to pour a few ounces of petrol into the aperture, wedged open by a piece of bamboo, and then gun the starter. These first-aid maneuvers always seemed to become necessary at the most inopportune moments, such as when the car was the only vehicle on a river crossing with a chain-operated ferry or on the late night return from some rugby match, usually in the dark, in the rain, with a post-celebration shaky hand.

Despite these expected minor setbacks, my adventure tracing the book's travels became a memorable, fascinating journey. The book's route from Kuala Lumpur followed the tortuous hill-climb pass over the central mountainous spine of peninsular Malaya. I could visualize the suffering of the starving, sick, desolate group as they struggled on foot up the unrelenting steep slopes of the Bentong Pass. That route would subsequently be the site of frequent ambushes of Commonwealth troops in the fourteen-year guerilla jungle warfare with Communist forces from 1947 to 1961.

Nevil Shute had done outstanding research on the various small fishing villages in his story. I was convinced that those I stopped at were the true locations visited by the dwindling survivors of that terrible march. To get into the feel of the settings Shute had described, I occasionally stayed overnight at the edge of the little settlements, and endured sleeping in the Rover that proved to be far from mosquito-proof. Some of the tiny places I stopped in probably hadn't seen a Caucasian for years, but the residents were consistently welcoming and no doubt highly entertained by my attempts at speaking Scot's-accented Malay. They always cheered when I joined them on their dusty outdoor, floodlit badminton courts where I was usually severely defeated by the youngsters. Crossing on some of the local ferries, the sight of the solitary Rover surrounded by the wide-eyed local inhabitants, was a joy to me. The ancient motor seemed to sit up proudly making the most of its unaccustomed popularity.

The experiences were not, however, always positive. On one occasion after several days of dust, sweat and overnight car camping, I sought the comforts of a small government sponsored guesthouse, sort of a motel. It was very modest accommodation, but had shower facilities that I desperately needed. There was a level of hesitation and stress visible as I asked for a room, but I was placated with the offering of a cold beer while the unit was prepared. My inadequate skill with the language kept me from understanding the cause of the delay. Only the next morning at breakfast I fathomed out that some traveling Indian businessman had been ejected from the accommodations to make space for the Tuan, the white man. I was not proud to be British that day.

The long single-track road passed through rice paddy fields, and was wedged between rubber plantations and the endless beaches of the South China Sea. The midday sun scorched incessantly, and with no food or water available for miles on end, I had clear, soul-searching visions of the wartime travels of those poor women and children twenty years earlier. I poured over the book each evening and immersed myself in a compassionate re-reading of their plight.

I dilly-dallied my way north to Kota Bahru following the fictitious travels. KB as it was called, at the northeast limit of Malaya, is named after a similarly geographically placed city in Britain. Some far-from-home early colonial settler from Newcastle, England no doubt chose to name it after his ancestral home.

Time had run out for my leave from the army so I had to rush the return, nearly four hundred miles back to Kuala Lumpur. I passed the journey in a deep reflective mindset, realizing that my three-day car trip represented one-third of the distance walked by the survivors during only their last ten months of suffering.

Immediately upon my return to K.L., I started planning my next trip. I wanted to follow the second half of the book, set in Australia. I had ample leave coming up ahead. One of the perks of a three-year posting to the Orient was the liberal, 'local' leave allowance, six weeks each year.

The focal point of my Australian trip was of course, Alice Springs, a small town in the heart of the continent, surrounded by baking desert, a thousand miles from any coastline. Prior to reaching Alice, I planned to visit my step-sister, Margaret, and her family in Southern Australia during a month long, three-thousand mile, 'walk-about' in Oz.

With book in hand, my adventure began on what was described as an 'indulgence' flight from Singapore to Darwin. This air travel was offered to service personnel and families of the Commonwealth Brigade in Malaya allowing them to make amazingly inexpensive journeys to Australia and New Zealand aboard military aircraft. The flights cost only about twenty dollars for standby availability. There were two inflexible criteria involved: Each passenger had to prove he had sufficient funds to pay for his civilian return fare if no military flight was available; and all military passengers were required to wear their official uniform en route, overflying Brunei which was yet again designated an active service (war) zone.

Landing safely in Darwin, I was blissfully unaware of its wartime bombarding by the Japanese. I had to wait another forty years to learn of that tragedy in Hugh Jackman and Nicole Kidman's depiction of the events in the great epic movie, 'Australia'.

After an overnight stay in a Darwin hotel, not budgeted in my financial calculations, my journey continued on a Royal New Zealand Air Force cargo plane to Brisbane. From there, I flew by civilian flight to Sydney, in much greater comfort and without the need for ear mufflers required on the previous twelve hours from Singapore. Sadly, budget and time constraints only allowed a two day stay in Sydney, but I did manage to visit many sights in that beautiful city, amazed by its size, although then it was only half of its present day population.

Map in hand, I took bus transportation to the extreme south of Sydney. The depot was still more than two miles from the start of open country. Overloaded with a huge rucksack, I set off to hitchhike almost one thousand miles to Adelaide. It was a scorching day, the beginning of four weeks of blistering heat. The pack became heavier with each step, and for a mile and a half there was definitely more hiking than hitching. With open country stretching ahead, I sat in the shade of a storefront pondering my next move.

Looking through the rather oily window, I realized the shop was a dilapidated used-car sales office. Traffic was close to non-existent on the road so I dumped my luggage and ambled into the showroom, although it hardly deserved that description.

The paunchy proprietor/sales person gave me the classic, "G' dai mate, what can I do you for?" Wondering if the linguistic reversal had been in jest or an omen of what was about to happen, my inquiry about the chances of hitchhiking out west brought forth a howl of laughter and a blunt, "Not a snowball's chance in hell!"

He leaned casually against one of the three semi-derelict cars in his establishment and said, "Not to worry, I've got the perfect solution to your problem."

With a flamboyant wave, I was directed to a late 40's Austin Seven. After a not-so-subtle appraisal of my financial status, he offered, with a leering smile, "Forty quid and drive her away."

I was between a rock and a hard place. My brief questioning on the machine's reliability brought forth an accusatory, offended act. "Do I look like the kind of bloke who'd sell you a 'dud' vehicle?"

Before I could summon a response, he sealed the deal with, "Tell you what, I'll change the battery to a fully charged one. They get a bit run down when they've sat for a while, unused."

I peeled off an alarmingly large number of one-pound notes, (it was long before the emergence of the Visa card). By now we were on first name terms and Bert's benevolence knew no limit. He put a couple of gallons of petrol in the tank, free of charge, and offered an empty, rusty, spare fuel-can saying, " It's a fair stretch between fill-ups out there, Mate!"

The little engine started reluctantly, with an accompanying blast of foul, black smoke. I didn't dare look back in case the former owner was rolling on the ground in fits of laughter at the luck he'd had disposing of the A7.

'Go west young man!' seemed to be the theme for the day, so with my rucksack almost filling the backseat, my walk-about adventure started. Struggling over the inclines of the coastal ridge, the wee car wasn't too enthused to go faster than forty miles per hour and it dawned on me that my planned two hundred miles per day was a bit optimistic. Stopping briefly for a mid-afternoon cup of tea and a meat pie, I soldiered on at a disappointing pace. That was a providential intake of sustenance because the day sped past faster than my hoped-for miles. Tired and hungry I stopped in Yass. The grub shops were closed so I took refuge in a little pub where I proved my foreigner status to the hilarity of the bar hangers.

I asked for a small beer. "Pony or Middie?" the smiling barmaid asked.

Taken aback, I almost bombed by saying, "Oh, I'm driving an Austin 7," thinking she was asking me if I'd come on a horse. Luckily, just in time I figured it out and pointed to the small five-ounce glass of the big guy on the next stool.

She poured my drink and filled up his almost empty glass. "G'dai, good on you mate, cheers," my new drinking pal said as he half emptied the glass in one swig.

By the time I'd sampled a few sips, his glass clinked on the bar top. "And again," he said.

The bar girl complied as my dusty friend and I got into conversation. During half a dozen glasses in the next twenty minutes, I gained a lot of vital news about the road ahead, none of it reassuring: "There's some long empty stretches and watch for roos."

I managed to extricate myself from the now crowded and smoke-filled saloon and hesitantly started up the car. It spluttered a bit but grudgingly moved into the empty road. A dusty, sparsely-treed pull-off thirty miles west was my overnight semi-hidden parking spot. The car had now met both transportation and accommodation needs.

Next morning, an hour further west, I located an isolated café and petrol pump. Tank filled, an emergency two gallons slopping in the rusty can, and a huge modestly priced breakfast inside me, I set off on the next two hundred mile stretch with optimism. I was seriously hung up in Gundegai, a quaint little place on the headwaters of the Murrumbidgee River. Absorbing the lore of 'the dog and the tucker box' of the old 'Waltzing Matilda' campfire song, I dilly-dallied longer than I should have. Crawling on at my top speed, dawdling in Wagga Wagga, I finally stopped for a fill-up at Darlington Point, which had a small garage and a hand-pump petrol outlet. There wasn't a great deal more at that intersection of two roads, but it was memorable because that's where the little Austin first became temperamental.

Restarting efforts resulted in a disconcerting slow turn of the engine, which became even frailer with subsequent attempts. The mechanic owner of the shop gave me his sad verdict. "Sounds like your battery's flat."

"It can't be," I whined. "It was fully charged just yesterday morning." I refrained from disclosing that was when I'd bought the car.

"Let's see if it will clutch start, " he advised. Sitting in the driver's seat, in gear and clutch rammed to the floor, I sweated anxiously while he did a stalwart job of pushing me along. Obligingly, the engine caught at the first try. I parked, but didn't dare switch off as I asked my rescue man for his advice.

"Sounds like your generator has packed in."

Alarmed I asked how much that would cost. "Oh, maybe a tenner and a couple of quid to install, but it'll take a few days to get a second-hand one sent out here."

He saw my horrified look, and consoled me with a glimmer of hope. "If you park on a slope, you should be able to do a run-start. They might have a spare in Mildura if you get that far." He was talking about the next fair-sized town, two hundred miles down the road.

I set off west toward the horizon twenty miles away, every inch as flat as a billiard table. A forty mile jaunt brought me to Hay, where to my delight I found a short steep bank with a trail down to the river. I parked on the slope, with hand brake fiercely wrenched to maximum, wedged two big rocks in front of the wheels, and treated myself to a snack in the café.

Asking the usual touristy questions, I found out that there was a good show at the theatre that night. It was almost dark and a quick look at the fairly elaborate façade of the place, dictated my return to the car to change into my only clean shirt and long pants. Dressed appropriately, I thought, I paid my shilling and passed through the front door to fetch up with surprise. It was an open-air cinema with long double-deck chair seating. Most of the spots were filled with 'courting couples' and I was the centre of attention and entertainment as I found the only vacant spot in the front row. Glaringly overdressed in that T-shirt and shorts-attired audience, I hunched down low as the catcalls and wolf whistles subsided. At the end of the show, I pretended to have fallen asleep until the place emptied, and then high-tailed it to the privacy of my four wheeled sleeping accommodation.

Next morning early, the A7 obligingly fired up without too much fuss before I hit the bottom of the slope. I pressed on west not daring to stop for sightseeing, and completed the trip to Mildura by early afternoon. I located a convenient parking slope on the edge of town. Being now well Aussified, I caught a spot of grub and checked out the garage.

"Sure, fifteen quid plus installation, maybe by tomorrow night," didn't appeal to me, so I moved on.

I'd covered another hundred miles when trouble hit again. It was a lovely little place, except that in the fast fading sunset, I couldn't find any vestige of a slope. I filled up the tank, not daring to switch off the engine and eased out into the darkness. A few miles out of town, behind a painted white fence, I spied an incline on an asphalted driveway leading into obviously private property. A little copse offered a hiding spot so I pulled in. Three hours of somewhat mosquito-disturbed sleep ended with peremptory ejection by two unfriendly policemen. The little A7 sensing the hostility, fired up obligingly on the down slope.

I drove almost non-stop for the next forty hours, totally spooked by events. I dragged into Whyalla on the other side of Spencer Gulf, past Adelaide, where Margaret and her family welcomed and nurtured me. They even tolerated my dumping of the A7 in their back land with my hope they might get a few bob for it. I was sad to leave the stalwart little transport. I would have liked to see the surprise on Bert's face, back in Sydney, if he had known I'd travelled one thousand miles in his 'reliable' vehicle.

Travelling up by air to the focal point of my Aussie tour, Alice Springs, I sat beside a grand old mature lady who was a total chatterbox. Of course, she'd met her match in me so the two of us got on like old pals in the five-hour flight. Her name was Mary and by the time we'd landed, it was established that I'd stay in the guest cabin near her residence in the permanent Aboriginal Old Timers' camp just outside of town. I'd told her of my desire to follow the path of Nevil Shute's book and she filled me in on the excitement the novel had brought to Alice Springs.

My visit completely fulfilled my dream of retracing the story. The time there also gave me insights into the unpublicized plight of the indigenous peoples of Australia in the 60's. At a later date, I was able to draw comparisons between the experience of the aboriginal people in Australia and the aboriginal people in Canada post European contact.

The residents of the Old Timers' Home lived in small individual, almost henhouse-like cabins, with their own private little garden area marked off with a string fence-line. They were curious about the new young fellow that Matron Mary escorted around. I was unable to communicate with them but my host translated for me. One day, I was wearing my army shorts and a T-shirt that, despite my protests, Mary had washed and ironed. An old resident approached me at his little fence. Mary was intrigued. "He never comes out to see strangers," she told me. He slowly came to the fence line and I saw the most amazing smile on his wrinkled face.

"He thinks that the creases on your shorts might cut him," she explained. He sat down on his heels and rocked back and forth, chuckling all the while. Finally he touched the sharp, starched creases with his gnarled finger. His disdain was evident; no doubt he was amazed at my foolishness to dress like that.

In my four short days there, I turned down an opportunity to travel to one of Australia's world famous tourist attractions, Ayer's Rock, just a hundred miles away. I was gaining so much of what I'd come to see and learn about, right in Alice.

All too quickly, it was over, and I had to fly north another thousand miles above the lonely beauty of the semi-barren, but historical, outback country. My window seat allowed me to absorb the terrain so meticulously portrayed in the story.

Landing at Darwin, it was once again back to reality. I enquired about the availability of an indulgence flight to Singapore. It was of little assurance to be told, "It's a day-to-day thing, come back in the morning."

Hoarding the required civilian airfare money, I was down to desperate lean times financially. I found an ultra modest, almost seedy room for the night, went on a starvation diet, and hitchhiked back to the air force base early the next day. There was a plane coming in from Brisbane in the afternoon, but it seemed that all seats were filled. To break the tedium, I managed to get up into the military control tower to watch the arrivals and departures. My bedraggled uniform and my story started to get their sympathy. The radio crackled and afterwards the chief laughed and explained, "You're lucky, three sailors missed their ship in Sydney and they are being dropped off here. You'll get a seat."

For the ten-hour flight north, I had wonderful memories of my glorious Australian walk-about, and a life-long appreciation of *A Town Like Alice*.

B.M.H. Cameron Highlands

*M*alaya was described by early European settlers as being always green and beautiful. There are a thousand species of flowering plants, ferns and trees, some of which tower two hundred feet, and are inhabited by hundreds of different species of birds and a similar variety of butterflies. Orchid hedgerows, bananas, pineapples, durian, papaya and coconuts to be picked by the roadside, make it sound like heaven on earth.

Much of Malaya is naturally exotic and fascinating, but the unrelenting heat and humidity, and lack of climatic change, wear down the visitor accustomed to four seasons. Consequently, just as Canadian 'snowbirds' head south for relief from the cold of winter, so too the reverse attraction draws holiday-makers away from the torrid heat of the lowlands. They seek respite in cool places in the six-hundred mile long Oriental Peninsula, the backbone of Malaya, which reaches over seven thousand feet in altitude.

Cameron Highlands is one of several mountain refuges located in this region. Originally described by British surveyor William Cameron in 1885, it was called the 'Soul of Malaya' by an early visitor. The almost-British temperatures year round provided relief from the torrid lowlands for the heat-exhausted Caucasians who, if they could, made yearly pilgrimages to convalesce and rejuvenate. In their few weeks' vacation, cooling off in the seventy-five degree Fahrenheit maximum temperatures, they tended to overlook the less appealing features of the place. Thousands of acres of tea plantations terraced on the slopes, and wall to wall commercial gardens are nurtured by the over two hundred inches of annual rainfall. A myriad of animal and insect life such as panthers, orang-utan, tapir, two hundred species of snakes, centipedes and other insects also presented potentially unpleasant encounters, although in their jungle home those creatures were seldom observed by the invading homo-sapiens.

After two years of unrelenting heat at Kinrara, near Kuala Lumpur, the offer of a posting to B.M.H. Cameron Highlands was answered with an almost down-on-the-knees, "Yes, please." I couldn't believe my good fortune. I'd heard great things about this place from patients who had gone there to convalesce, and from some hospital staff who had enjoyed restorative holidays there with their families.

To add incentive (though none was needed) the C.O. informed me that I'd been chosen to open a new Physical Rehabilitation Centre in the Highlands. Memories of fitness tests and 'tenting' shortcomings were apparently forgotten. I went through the customary jettisoning of accumulated excess baggage, and survived the traditional overindulgent farewell send-off party. It was with mixed emotions that I left the place I'd called home for two years, and the many special friends I had made there.

Little Vespa was super-loaded with a box strapped to the pannier frame at the back and an equally heavy suitcase straddling the foot-well in front of the seat. Overflow items of clothing and other paraphernalia filled a rucksack that nearly upset my precarious balance as I sat astride my faithful machine. Of course, the opportunity to enhance my tan on the five hour trip dictated that all I wore was a pair of skimpy shorts and sandals. The mess staff came out to send me off, with the same smiles and kindness with which they'd welcomed me two years earlier. It wasn't macho to cry at such moments, but there was a tear in my eye as I gave each of them a hug.

I had much to reminisce about during the hundred mile trip to Tapah, the main coastal town before the mountains. After a brief pit stop, I added a layer of long pants and a long-sleeved shirt in readiness for the one degree Fahrenheit drop in temperature per mile of the hill climb.

It was hard to imagine that just three years earlier all travellers on this road would have made the journey in a convoy accompanied by mandatory armed servicemen. The road, twisting and turning as it edged up the mountain, squeezed through overhanging jungle on one side and precipitous drops on the other. It had been a favourite site for ambushes by Communist terrorists attacking Commonwealth military trucks during the fourteen-year guerrilla war that had only ended recently. Small marker-crosses still identified spots where many young soldiers had given their lives.

Greater realization of the contribution made by these soldiers and those who survived the emergency came to me 50 years later when I was presented with my PJM medal (Pingat Jasa Malaysia). This medal recognized service by the peacekeeping troops during the period of the emergency and confrontation. At the ceremony were very emotional former servicemen who had tears in their eyes and shaking voices as they described that period of history. I felt less deserving of the medal as I personally never faced the terrorist threat.

An hour later, and only twenty miles up the hill, I had to put on the next layer of clothing. I had forgotten what a sweater felt like, but needed the extra warmth it gave to combat the dropping temperature. Ten more miles along the road, the rain started. Only those who have experienced a monsoon deluge will understand that feeling. The British Army poncho is supposedly waterproof, but that does not guarantee a dry ride on a Vespa.

Weight, water and weariness of that final half-hour of the journey made me a sad sight to see on my tottering arrival in front of B.M.H. Cameron Highlands. I was observed with interest by a small group nestled comfortably in the arched foyer of the hospital, enjoying an afternoon cup of tea. My attempts to park my overloaded bike failed miserably. It crashed onto its side toppling its cargo and rider. This was not an auspicious entrance, but was greeted with sympathetic smiles by the audience who were none other than the C.O., the Matron and two nurses.

"You'll be the new Physiotherapy Sergeant," the C.O. guessed, seizing my soaking hand. He introduced me to the others at the tea-party. I got an instant inkling of the friendly atmosphere as he said, "Park your machine in that alcove, and I'll show you the way to the Sergeants' Mess."

Weighted down with my water-logged rucksack, I followed his loping gait up two flights of steps and along a corridor. I was intrigued by his Irish accent and idiom as he painted a rosy picture of the ambiance of the place and staff. He swung open the door to a cozy little sitting room where four senior non-commissioned officers, the entire compliment, were halfway through their afternoon pints. Nobody leapt to their feet as the C.O. introduced me, simultaneously opening the refrigerator to haul out two pint bottles. "Put these on my tab," he said, confirming that he enjoyed 'Honorary Membership' status in the Sergeants' Mess.

I was shown the modest little room that would be my home for the next year. Dressed in dry clothes, I returned to the group and quickly become aware of the comfortable camaraderie. Half an hour later, his pint consumed, the C.O. departed, reaffirming his welcome and casualness. "The boys here," meaning the other mess residents, "will show you where to park your motor scooter and help you with your baggage. See if you can catch up with me in the morning and I'll give you a full tour of the place." This was far more informal than the relationship I'd had with my previous C.O. in Kinrara.

By the time my new associates had helped me lug the rest of my worldly goods to the room, the evening meal had been brought up from the hospital kitchen. We had individual trays with steaming-hot plates under metal covers. As each item appeared, I was amazed at the size of the portions, they were huge. My surprise showed. "We're all on 'arduous rations' because this is a rehabilitation hospital," the Company Sergeant Major (C.S.M.) informed me. "Everybody gets almost twice the normal calorie level, to build them up. These big meals are intended to compensate for all the exercise we do up here." He was a lanky forty year old who could eat and drink any amount without putting on an extra pound. He gave a scornful look at two of the other Sergeants who were noticeably rotund. I subsequently learned that they had sedentary clerical jobs and never raised a sweat in any physical endeavour.

The next day I got a 'Royal Tour' of the place. The ground floor of the former convent school was occupied with offices and storerooms, a tiny x-ray department with antique equipment, kitchen facilities and a dining room for staff and patients. A steep flight of stairs opened onto a corridor leading to three, small, twenty-bed wards. "You'll be excited to see your re-hab-il-it-ation department," the C.O. said, as we mounted another flight of steps. His accent broke the word into five separate syllables.

He pushed open a set of double doors with a great flourish and swept into the vacant 30'x20' high-ceilinged room. "Isn't she a beauty," he said, 'but that's only the half of it." At the opposite end of that barren space a short corridor led to more steps up to a similarly-sized room, equally devoid of furnishings. "So, what do you think then?" he asked.

It took me a moment to find words but finally I managed, "It's a lot of space, but where is the equipment?"

He looked me in the eye. "I have it on good authority from Kinrara that you are a man of amazing ingenuity and perseverance. I'm sure you'll be able to improvise. Just scribble a list of things you can't make and we'll send off for them. It might take a while for things to arrive, but just make do in the meantime."

That settled, he spun on his heel and led the way back down the seemingly interminable steps. "Oh, by the way, the main priority of the day is at three o'clock. I hear tell you're a dab-hand at badminton, so book the court for my game with you this afternoon. Just get settled in."

Badminton aside (and he was a good opponent), the opportunity to create an entirely new rehab centre was an enviable, but somewhat mindboggling, proposition. There I was, twenty-three years old, being given a free hand to start from bare walls and execute the project. That first week I talked with everyone who would listen and give me their ideas about the place. Other than the one central badminton court, the amenities included only a small library and a cinema where the once-per-week show filled every seat. The Naafi canteen had a couple of table-tennis tables and a snooker table.

The sixty or so patients had all been referred to B.M.H. Cameron Highlands from other military hospitals. The patients were ambulatory but had a wide range of medical and surgical conditions causing their on-going need for hospitalisation. Their acute care had progressed sufficiently to make them candidates for a final few weeks of intermediary care and rehabilitation prior to returning to full duties in their individual Army, Navy, or Air Force units. A number of the patients were in the final recovery stages following fractures, sprains, knee cartilage repairs, and neck and back injuries, all similar to cases I'd been treating routinely in Kinrara. There were, however, numerous medical patients who had suffered debilitating diseases common in the tropics. These included malaria, tuberculosis, liver, kidney and lung disorders that brought about disastrous weight loss and weakness. I spent time with almost every patient that first week, learning their medical histories and finding out what they'd be expected to do on return to their units. It was a most enlightening experience for me, and helped give me ideas for the role I could play in their recovery.

I got support from all the other staff members, and interesting ideas to pursue. The C.S.M.., a real 'old soldier', had the most practical advice. When I asked where I might find rudimentary items such as ropes, footballs, and basketballs, he suggested I pay a visit to the nearby 'Change of Air' camp. The camp was a group of Nissan huts located a hundred yards from the hospital. The huts accommodated about one hundred soldiers from units all over Malaya on two week rotations. These personnel spent time on light duty as a rejuvenation period in the cool air of the Highlands. The C.S.M. advised, "Visit on their changeover day. There'll be only three or four blokes left there at that time so go beg, borrow, or steal anything you can lay your hands on. If they ask what you are doing say the C.O. ordered the transfers." I was dubious about these recommendations but got a surprise welcome and was given a free hand to load a jeep with all sorts of treasures. It was a great start and helped change my two empty caverns into some semblance of an exercise department.

The hospital had a small workshop intended as a place for the unit engineering staff to do maintenance and repairs. Patients with carpentry skills, with the C.O.'s 'authorization' of course, took over the area and made exercise benches and treatment couches with materials that were scrounged from the most unlikely sources. Gradually, over several months, some of the equipment I'd scribbled on my list of urgent needs trickled in from other hospitals in the country. I suspected, judging by the state of these pieces, that they were items that had been replaced with newer models and so were generously passed along. I felt a true sense of satisfaction and pride as I saw the rehabilitation centre taking shape.

There were, of course, moments of frustration bordering on the absurd. Just before my scheduled departure for the UK at the end of my year in the Highlands, news came that a large casement of medical equipment was at the Tapah railway station. I couldn't imagine what it might be but I was very excited about the prospects. Such a precious load justified a day's outing to collect the treasure. All the way down the hill I chatted with the Malay driver of our three-ton truck, racking my brain trying to remember what else I'd put on my original list. It took four helpers to load the huge wooden crate. There wasn't a hint about its contents except for the multiple glaring stickers: "Handle With Care. Medical Equipment."

Our arrival back at the hospital parking lot was met with pent-up excitement. Half the hospital turned out, and many willing hands joined in the unveiling. It was the most dramatic moment the place had seen in months. The whole crowd cheered when the final wrappings were torn off. Silence followed as we viewed the brand new, never been touched, set of exercise steps with their high-gloss wooden railings. This was definitely not from any list I had made. The attached packing slip indicated the place of origin as the medical equipment depot in London. The army had done it again. The dispatcher in the UK obviously hadn't heard that B.M.H. Cameron Highlands was perched precariously on a steep mountain-side in Malaya, and that nearly every step taken there was up or down. I took a lot of ribbing about that step-training equipment, but a few beers later it seemed almost funny.

At the back of the hospital an expanse of paved, rare, flat ground had been gouged out of the surrounding jungle. Originally it had been an overflow parking area for convoys of trucks dating back to when the Japanese army had taken over the original buildings to create a hospital during their invasion of Malaya in World War II. One of my first projects was to install removable volleyball and basketball posts and nets in the pavement. The patients clamoured to help and worked with picks and shovels with gusto. Once they had an idea of what was needed, a group of Gurkhas disappeared into the surrounding jungle and emerged in no time with the required bamboo posts. Paint was procured and willing hands measured and outlined the courts. Play was started almost before the paint was dry. As weather permitted, teams competed constantly, and it wasn't an uncommon sight to see enthusiasts defy the elements and splash around basketball hoops even in the torrential rain.

As I got a better grasp of the range of fitness of the patients, early morning hikes down the main road became part of the treatment for most of them. Single file we'd walk downhill for twenty-five minutes, take a five minute breather, then push the pace on the return journey to get back up the gradient within the hour. In the early afternoons I'd take a dozen or so of the high-performance lads, who were nearly ready to return to their units, to the stepped benches of the tea plantations. We'd climb five hundred feet up through these terraces, a strenuous exercise for even the very fit.

The challenge of these sessions provided an important boost to the self-confidence of these fellows. Some of them had endured months of hospitalization.

The most memorable feature of B.M.H. Cameron Highlands was the close camaraderie I had experienced from day one, in that isolated outpost of the Empire. With a total staff of only forty, we soon got to know each other well and were a mutually supportive extended family. There were some real characters in that group and I learned a lot about life, including a tolerance for others' foibles and idiosyncrasies.

In the Sergeants' Mess, the five live-in members were about as different as individuals could be. On my arrival one of the chaps showed enthusiasm that I was a Scot. He envisioned me as a ready companion to share his delight in the midnight playing of his four scratchy-sounding records on an ancient gramophone. They were all recordings by Kenneth McKellor, the great Scottish tenor. I did enjoy the first couple of songs on the first record, but hearing those midnight renditions a couple of times a week for a year put me off that talented singer for a lifetime.   Enquiring about the appropriateness of playing music at that late hour, the C.S.M. advised me to get ear plugs if it bothered me. I protested and asked why nobody had sabotaged the records. "Don't even think about that," he said. "A happy chap is better than an angry one, so that subject is now closed." His cautioning came from the wisdom of his years and experience. Hearing the seriousness of his tone, I learned to live with the situation, as the other residents had done.

The C.S.M. had his own unique habit. He was an obsessive reader. He consumed two or three novels each week and could pursue prolonged, meaningful conversations with those around him without impeding his page turning every minute or so. The other mess members had their habits too. One was hooked on the card game, 'Patience'. He played by the hour and seemed oblivious to any distracting happenings in his surroundings. Another, a bit of a loner, played his guitar endlessly, but quietly, in his room. He kept a pet python, just three feet long. It was in a cage most of the time but he did let it out to play from time to time and would wander into the lounge to get a tin of pop from the fridge with the darn snake coiled around his arm. I seemed to contribute a model of traditional and normal lifestyle to the mess, although 'normal' was obviously subjective. I once overheard a conversation that wasn't intended for my ears, but was definitely about me. "That new guy is totally insane. He's a bloody exercise freak, and he chases women and he can eat like a horse. I know he eats my supper as well as his own." The fact that most of it was true took some of the edge off the criticism.

I did play badminton every day, and organized and joined in on the regular games of volleyball and basketball. Soccer too was still one of my passions. We had a regular 'Brit' team made up of hospital staff and a few of the healthier patients. We'd play against the village team of multinational make-up, including Malay, Chinese and Indian. Often one of those happy-go-lucky enthusiasts would choose to play in bare feet and could kick the ball as far as his boot wearing opposition. At practice sessions I tried the barefoot approach, much to the hilarity of the locals. Overtime, I got better at that skill and found it greatly improved my technique. Years later I recall horrifying parents of soccer teams that I coached. Having just spent outlandish amounts for their child's new boots, the mums and dads were up-in-arms when I got the kids to remove their soccer boots so that they could learn to kick the ball properly in bare feet. It was a great way to stop the toe-kick habit.

Another contributing factor to my 'exercise freak' description was my delight in hiking the well-marked jungle trails up the mountains to their seven thousand foot peaks. The narrow pathways were well maintained by the shy indigenous Sakai tribesmen. These mountain people avoided contact with visitors, and their natural camouflage of dress and skin colour made them almost undetectable even at close range in their jungle habitat. On one hike with a group from the hospital, we stopped to observe a large, harmless monitor lizard sitting at the edge of the thick foliage. As the others moved on, I was having one last look at the lizard when my eye caught the outline of the foot of one of the natives. He had been standing still and silent inches from us, camouflaged in the surrounding jungle fronds.

That mountain landscape was truly a place of beauty. Lush greenery, trees, bushes, ferns, interspersed with exotic plants and flowers. Butterflies of every imaginable shape and colour, and birds of every variety, filled those paths with buzzing and humming and a rainbow of hues. Often we'd be caught in torrential downpours on our hikes. We'd start off in brilliant sunshine with a cloudless-sky and within one hour we'd be soaked. A bonus of the heavy rains was the resulting rushing streams, waterfalls and pools, and a dazzling array of fish that could be seen in the clear water.

Some members of the permanent staff at the hospital did suffer 'cabin or mountain' fever, (a mild depression) when the whole area was shrouded with impenetrable cloud for days on end. I was fortunate to be able to do a reverse 'Change of Air' every couple of months or so, freewheeling downhill on the Vespa to the heat and sunshine of tropical beaches for a few days.

As I write these pages, my heart is pounding and an irrepressible smile has crept onto my face, remembering my glorious year on the 'roof-top' of Malaya, half a century ago. Only a Scot could have named the place so appropriately, the Cameron Highlands.

The Two Soldiers

*E*ven the utopian Cameron Highlands had times of unpleasant weather. In October that small community, primarily the British Military Hospital, in northern Malaya suffered the onslaught of the monsoon season. The towering jungle-clad mountains became shrouded in perpetual cloud. What was otherwise a much sought after idyllic retreat, became a grey, cold, unrelentingly wet land that invited escape for those residents who had the opportunity to do so.

In November 1963, it became my turn to go 'down the hill' as the holiday was often described. With great excitement I ventured onto the forty-mile zigzagged narrow road to the refreshing heat and sunshine of the lowlands. The first leg of the journey, on my trusty 125cc Vespa scooter, was a two-day, four hundred mile trip to Singapore through Tapah, Slim River, and Kuala Lumpur. I followed the same road the Japanese invading armies had traveled on twenty years earlier. Their mission was to capture Singapore, the fortified port that has been pronounced impregnable from the sea. The overland invasion, down peninsular Malaya, proved a sad oversight in the defense of that gem of the British Empire.

In Singapore I boarded a cruise ship that took me to such intriguing venues as Saigon, Hong Kong and Japan. The ship, somewhat less splendid than today's floating, five thousand person mini-cities, was with the Messageries Maritimes Cargo/Passenger line. My journey was part of its routine voyage traveling halfway across the world from Marseilles to Tokyo. The Laos, the steamship I was on, carrying a mere two hundred passengers, departed from Singapore on the twentieth of November. The shared tourist cabin that I occupied was far more modest than today's luxurious staterooms, but the price was right. I quickly settled in to leisurely tourist bliss and reveled in sitting on the open deck, beer in hand without a concern in the world. As I lay on the deck chair in my shorts, glorying in the delights of sunbathing and socializing, I felt real joy in this unexpected opportunity for a twenty-four year old British Army Sergeant.

In graphic contrast, nearby, another twenty-four year old soldier was in very different circumstances. Lieutenant Nick Rowe, a US Special Forces Green Beret, was in the 'Plain of Reeds', a flat, mosquito-ridden, swampy area of the Mekong Delta. Three weeks earlier his platoon, involved in training South Vietnamese Army Rangers, had been ambushed. The Viet Cong captured him and two other Americans. He was imprisoned in a bamboo cage, often submerged with only his head above the snake-infested waters. His captors interrogated him continually, trying to obtain information about US military maneuvers in the area. His life was one of harassment, sleep deprivation, disease and malnutrition. It was early days in the Vietnam saga and American troops were still described as 'advisors' to the South Vietnamese Army. War had not yet been declared.

I am embarrassed to admit that as a young British soldier enjoying a posting in far off Malaya, I was greatly lacking in knowledge of what was happening in Vietnam in November 1963. In the Cameron Highlands at that time, there was no English TV, virtually no world news, and scant awareness of world affairs outside the realm of our secluded little hospital environment. I was blithely unaware that there were already thousands of American service personnel in South Vietnam.

My education was about to improve, as the first port of call on our cruise was Saigon. Entry into that city involved four hours of very slow sailing along the confining banks of the Mekong River as it meandered its way through the delta to the South China Sea. One hour before our docking in Saigon the Captain made a somber announcement: "Mesdames and Messieurs, this is your Captain. I am very sad to announce that President Kennedy of the United States has been assassinated."

The few American passengers on the open decks showed shock and instant grief at the news. The remainder, many British, Australians and other nationalities, although saddened weren't as deeply distressed. Like many, my ignorance of current affairs made it difficult to grasp the ramifications of that announcement.

"Furthermore," the Captain said, "we advise extreme caution if you choose to go ashore." Without more information forthcoming at that time, I couldn't understand why Saigon would be more dangerous than any other major city. It was known as the 'Paris of the East' with its boulevards, Citroen cars, and magnificent displays of French colonial architecture. I, of course, went ashore. Sadly lacking in knowledge of Saigon's history, I had anticipated a fully Asian atmosphere of trishaws, markets and the hustle bustle of the Orient. I was surprised and amazed by the French influence. France had been a major colonial power in Indo-China in the first half of the twentieth century. In Saigon, I enjoyed chatting with the locals in their common second language, French, although there was some inherent complication caused by my Scots-accented French and their oriental-nuanced version of that language.

Meanwhile back in his bamboo cage, Nick Rowe was simultaneously hearing the news of President Kennedy's assassination. Rowe's captors continually berated him for his supreme commander's involvement in that 'unjust war' on the Vietnamese Communist regime. Trying to weaken his beliefs, they harangued him with reports of the anti-war demonstrations in the US. Now they described his President's death as 'justice' because of Kennedy's orders for military 'atrocities' in their country. Nick Rowe would soon feel the ramifications of the assassination. Within days of his appointment, President Johnson escalated the status of the US involvement in Vietnam from that of 'advisors' to a full declaration of war. This provoked greater abuse and maltreatment by Rowe's captors.

Oblivious to all of this during my thirty-six hours in Saigon, I continued my tourist travels with a visit to the magnificent presidential gardens known for their tropical flowers, trees and birds, and grand colonial-style architecture. Away from the hubbub of traffic, and the cacophony of language, scooters and horns, the tranquility of the gardens was beautiful. I marveled at the apparent peacefulness of the place despite the constant presence of military forces just outside the gates. As I went about my sightseeing, it became difficult to ignore the change in situation. I was staggered by the extent of the American military presence. Throughout that day, I gradually absorbed the importance of past history, and began to understand a little of what was presently unfolding in Saigon. I was on a fast learning curve.

The ship slowly made its return down the Mekong to continue the voyage to Hong Kong and Japan. As I relaxed on the deck, I was oblivious to Nick Rowe and others imprisoned a stone's throw away.

We made another two-day stop in Saigon on the return trip two weeks later. There was an even sterner caution from the Captain advising passengers of the grave dangers ashore. As with our first stop there, youthful exuberance and naivety dictated disregard for these warnings, and I again ventured ashore. There was an unimaginable change in the city. The American presence had significantly increased even in that short time.

When I was having a lovely meal in a roof-top garden restaurant in downtown Saigon, I was surprised to see what I thought was a fireworks display in the distance. I was shocked and sobered to find out that it was a full military assault on the sister city, Cholon, just six miles away. The ship was a welcome safe haven that night.

Next morning things seemed quieter and perhaps ominously so, but I made another trip to the presidential gardens I'd visited two weeks previously. I was horror-stricken at the sight. During my absence many of the buildings and gardens had been destroyed. The place was desolate. I again made a rapid return to the safety of the ship.

Nick Rowe had another five years to endure in captivity. He witnessed the death of several fellow prisoners; he suffered ill health, near starvation and unending physical and psychological abuse. It was constant angst for him to realize how close he was to other American service personnel as jets and helicopters passed over him daily.

When, years later, I read the gripping account of Nick Rowe's survival and eventual escape in *Five Years to Freedom,* I realized the irony of our circumstances. The disparity was sobering: That same November, in Vietnam, he in his bamboo cage, starving, and I, sitting on the deck of a cruise ship, sipping beer. Two young soldiers, so close yet so very far apart.

B.M.H. Iserlohn

*O*n my return from Malaya exactly three years to the day since my departure for the East, I was due, deserved or not, six weeks disembarkation leave, all of which I spent at home in Dumfries. My family were delighted to see me but mother had to quickly divest me of a few unacceptable lifestyle habits I'd adopted in Malaya. There, the Amah, or laundry lady had tolerated the young Sergeant's clothes-washing chores without complaint, at least none that I was aware of.

The daily routine had been get up in the morning, pull on a pair of shorts and a t-shirt and go for breakfast. Thereafter I'd get into a fresh starched uniform for parade and go to work. Obviously, it would be untidy to leave the shorts and t-shirt lying around, so the natural thing was to throw them into the laundry basket. By noon, that uniform was coated with sweat and needed laundering, necessitating a fresh outfit. After work at 3:30 pm, the next uniform also required cleaning, as did a pair of shorts worn to play a quick game of badminton before our football match at 5 pm. Football outfits do get sweaty so... Depending on how ambitious the evening socializing became one of two outfits usually finished off the day. The basket was always overflowing by bed time.

Mother took two days and one severe tongue lashing to eradicate that habit. Likewise, she speedily curtailed my enormous appetite that had kept up with my overindulgence of sports activities without producing an ounce of fat. I was the envy of all my chubby friends who just looked at food and put on weight. "You've eaten a weeks' worth of groceries in two days. Subject, closed and resolved," were her exact words.

I'd got Vespa 1 back on the road after its three-year rest during my absence and started late night jaunts to town. I was careful not to drink as that was an obvious no-no, but 2 am returns with the resultant late morning sleep in didn't go down well. I tried to negotiate. "I'm twenty-four years old," I pleaded.

"Aye and I'm nearly fifty-four and have to get up in the morning, so midnight return will be just fine," she said.

I'd come back totally bronzed by the sun, (well most of me), and that first weekend home was scorching, for Scotland. The early June temperature soared to seventy degrees Fahrenheit. The grassy bank at the swimming hole on the river sprouted the whitest bodies I'd ever seen. It was 1964, the era of Speedo swimming trunks, and my mahogany tan just had to be exposed. I disrobed, and hearing adoring sighs, and a few, "Bloody Hells," from the lads, I had no choice but to hit the water. Others were swimming around without complaint, but when I broke the surface after a majestic swallow dive, I nearly died. It was the briefest swim in history. I scrambled into my clothes, and peered back to verify that there really wasn't ice on the pool. I had obviously lost my tolerance for Scottish swimming conditions on the tropical beaches of Malaya.

I did quite a lot of work around the house and garden during those weeks at home, but I think mother and I were mutually relieved when I set off for my next posting in Germany.

In three days back at the Royal Army Medical Corp depot at Crookham, I got rid of my olive-green outfits and was refitted in classic British khaki battle dress uniform. I then flew from London to Dusseldorf. As soon as I was off the plane I saw a young lad with a large sign saying FARISH. This was unexpected, but soon explained: "It takes an hour to get to Iserlohn, and you are playing football ninety minutes from now." That I liked.

As we drove to my new home in the army jeep, I got caught up with the news of friends from the past who I'd met somewhere on my travels. Everything was laid on, so upon arrival at the base, I was bundled off to a local village to play against their football team.

A round ball, nine inches in diameter, does funny things to a football-crazy bunch. I had developed, amongst other skills, a super technique of a legal slide-tackle on the often slippery wet grass in Malaya. Old habits die hard and in my enthusiasm, and desire to impress my new team mates, I utilised that 'piece de resistance' in the first five minutes of play. Sadly, I'd not absorbed the fact that we were playing on a shale surface, not grass, and knee to buttock was rubbed raw on the unfriendly pitch surface. Stubbornly I leaked blood till the game was over, then with my leg wrapped tightly in a towel, joined in the post match refreshment in my first visit to a Gasthaus, (the local pub). Three hours later I was feeling no pain, conversing loudly if not intelligibly using all of the dozen German words I'd learned in that time. It was a great welcome to Germany and B.M.H. Iserlohn.

I limped into work next morning with miles of tensor bandage trying to stave off the blood seepage. My new boss was a mature Glasgow-born lady of some fifty plus vintage, Mrs. Johnson*. She obviously relished the idea that we spoke the same language, Scots, and was most welcoming and friendly. My other work colleague was a young Manchester girl, my age, with a wicked sense of humour. Within minutes she put the cards on the table with her straight talk.

"I'm engaged to a Canadian Artillery Captain," she announced, then in a stage-whisper added, "but I think the boss fancies you."

It was interesting getting into the routine of the hospital located in a former German Cavalry and Armoured Division Barracks. Built in the 1930's it was relatively new compared to some of the London hospitals. Converted into a British Military Hospital in 1946, its five blocks of three-story former accommodations provided fairly spacious wards, departments, and living quarters for Canadian and British medical and nursing staff. Stores, laundry and engineering departments were located in the former stables, and a huge gym complex was created from truck and tank garages. The aforementioned shale football pitch had been a vehicle parking lot and was still occasionally used as the landing zone for helicopters bringing in emergency patients. This facility gave a new rendition to the classic British cricket statement, 'rain stopped play', which became, 'chopper stops play', during our football matches.

Working with the Canadian staff was wonderfully rewarding. Some of Canada's great regiments were stationed within a sixty kilometre range in nearby Zoest, Wuppertal, and other townships, part of the military force B.A.O.R. (British Army On the Rhine). Of special intrigue were the 'Vandoos', the Royal Twenty-Second Regiment of Canada. As patients, they gave me my first connection with French Canadian soldiers. Many were proudly, and adamantly, unilingual in a version of the French language bearing no resemblance to the Parisian dialect I'd learned in school. They of course found my Scots-accented vocabulary equally incomprehensible. This often resulted in gales of laughter as I tried to lead them in exercise classes.

Sports, of course, were a part of unit life and the international mix brought about new and diverse activities. Two or three times each year we'd have a baseball-cricket match. This involved twenty over's of cricket and a similar set of baseball innings. It was hilarious to watch the rival teams trying to come to terms with the unaccustomed idiosyncrasies of the foreign game.

In Iserlohn I got my first exposure to curling. Living in the Sergeants' Mess, I was often called in as, 'spare' for the mess team.

My first attempt was less than stellar. Having experienced the shame of sliding my rock a mere fifteen feet from the hatch, I overcompensated with the typical explosive barn-clearing next shot. Eventually I was able to even things out, more or less. Quite different from most sports involving skill and accuracy, my curling game improved significantly in proportion to beer intake.

Early on in that first winter, I got away for a week and travelled to Austria to attend a ski-school. I loved skiing from the outset, which was another important element in the future move to Canada. Although Iserlohn is some distance from the mountains in Europe, a pleasant, modest ski area at Winterberg, only an hour away, became a regular weekend jaunt during much of my stay in Germany. I'd invested in wheels, namely a dilapidated Opal Caravan station wagon that tolerated the challenge of six bodies and their skis crammed inside, for those memorable excursions.

The countryside surrounding Iserlohn was part of the Ruhr waterways and industrial complexes. It had an ominous historical background. The entire area of the great hydroelectric plants and reservoirs was the focal point of the allied bombings portrayed in the 'Dam Busters' movie. Restored and manicured after the war, this location was a scenic tourist attraction, belying the horror of the war-time destruction of the Monashee and Zorpesee dams.

A number of German civilian staff were engaged in work at the hospital so a few close friendships inevitably developed. The Sergeants' Mess had a delightful elderly couple who worked in the kitchen. They often hosted the young live-in members almost as family, and introduced many Brits and Canadians to genuine German cooking. Those were evenings of delightful repartee, enhanced with often humorous linguistic challenges. This was a special, and unfortunately, unusual connection. As with military bases around the world, life at B.M.H. Iserlohn, although in a foreign country, day to day was British. Even when personnel did make social connections off the base, it was most often with members of the military from other near-by bases, rather than with members of the local population.

One memorable exception occurred when a pal and I stopped at a roadside and went into a field where a family was loading hay ricks onto carts. Our offer of 'two pairs of helpful hands' was welcomed, and we worked side-by-side for much of the afternoon. A subsequent invitation back to their farm for supper led to a special evening as their guests. Although their hosting of us was very genuine, there was suspicion from the elderly grandmother who just sat back observing the young 'foreigners'. She reminded me of my Nana's similar attitude twenty years earlier in Scotland, when the road-working German prisoners of war befriended me as a five year old. I have always been grateful that my friend and I made that effort of interaction, as it was one of the few times I had social contact with the local rural population of the area.

One memory shared by most members of the British and other military personnel stationed in Germany in the 1960's was the annual Octoberfest celebrations in the villages and towns amidst the large numbers of foreign bases. I recall a feeling of genuine welcome as we'd enter any of the Gasthaus pubs. At first it was a bit of a culture shock to be greeted by strangers with the classic, "Guten Abend," as soon as we got through the doorway. I took the memory of those warm welcomes away with me - a habit worth developing, a special touch that lingers from my posting at B.M.H. Iserlohn.

Good God

*G*od has had a long, perplexing connection with the Farish family. His forgiving nature has been evident throughout the last eight generations, and the family has been the benefactor of His goodness on countless occasions.

My first awareness of 'Church' was near the end of the war years when our attendance and involvement in the local Craig United Free Church was a fact of life, non -negotiable. That's what we did on Sundays.

A splinter group from the Church of Scotland, the Wee Free Kirk, as it was called, set up shop in their small granite edifice in 1844. The Farish carpentry firm was involved in its building and furnishing. A century later, the long wooden bench-seats and railings still showed the signs of hand–sawn and planed timber construction. Craftsmanship was evident in the rustic pews, well-worn doors, the engraving and fluting on the pulpit, and the stained glass windows. The slightly tattered and fading banner, spread almost full-width above the minister's perch, proclaimed for all to see, "Worship the Lord in the Beauty of Holiness."

My grandfather was an elder of the Kirk, and his contributions helped make the Wee Free welcoming and comfortable. In the 1920's he assisted with the installation of heating water pipes under the pews, bringing unheard of warmth to the congregation. The wood-fuelled boiler furnace had to be lit at 7 am on Sundays to ensure the church was warm enough for the early afternoon worship service.

By the early 1950's, the 'fire and brimstone' sermons had diminished as had the numbers of those attending. This almost merited the misquote: "Where two or three are gathered together there's plenty of room for Him in their midst." Our family, however, continued to attend.

The Farish pew, the last one on the left at the back, gave an enviable viewpoint to see who was in attendance. Dating back to times when families paid for their selected seating row, my cousin Neilson and I often wondered if we were in the cheap seats or the expensive ones.

One dear lady had somehow established herself in 'our' pew for reasons nobody ever explained to me. She was Bella, short for Isabella, small in stature, but magnificent of voice. She was the Wee Free version of Susan Boyle, two generations before that brilliant vocalist's time. Bella never missed a Sunday, rain or shine. She was a God-send, so to speak, because she had an unlimited supply of Scots peppermint sweets that she doled out generously to our row. That in itself made church attendance bearable for seven year olds.

I have many other fond memories of the Kirk that made regular visits enjoyable and almost fun. The organist was an ancient chap (probably younger than my present age) who fitted in splendidly with the musty décor. His bow tie always listing sideways, he'd start the antique metronome to give himself the beat. He'd then frantically try to keep up with its pace, often quite unsuccessfully, throughout each hymn. Another solitary elder statesman was a reliable part of the scenery, third row from the rear, on the right. He was totally deaf, but sang with discordant gusto, guessing the start and finish times of the hymns by watching others.

A dozen was a good turnout, the largest percentage being provided by the Farish clan. Uncle Joe was always last in and first out, befitting his shyness. Despite the brevity of his presence he did listen to the sermon. When I was a teenager he'd try to discuss a couple of points of the sermon with me. Of course, it was a lost cause. What thirteen year-old has ever listened to what was said, inside or outside of church? Uncle Dick, as a Deacon, stayed out to count the paltry few coins in the 'honour system' collection plate at the door before slipping into the seat beside us after the first hymn.

The poor minister soldiered on in God's work from the pulpit, a thankless task which he managed to smile through Sunday after Sunday. Our Wee Free shared him with another miniscule parish some miles away. Fortunately he could offer the same sermon to each micro-congregation.

That attendance at church in my youth gave me a rudimentary knowledge of the Bible and its teachings. In the family home at Broombrush, in my early years, the huge leather-bound ancestral Bible sat at rest after its over-use in the 1920's when my mother and my uncles were forced to endure my grandfather's protracted readings every night.

I learned virtually nothing during school morning prayers. Like the seven hundred other high-school students standing in the auditorium, I paid little attention to the poor fifteen year old stuttering through the Beatitudes. Likewise, the hymn-of-the day got lip-service at best.

The army didn't show much forgiveness in the matter of church attendance. The Church parade was printed on 'the day's orders', therefore you attended. It didn't take me long to catch onto the perfect excuse and avoidance scam. Most military services were geared for the predominantly Church of England majority. On the few occasions I was obliged to attend, I was ill at ease with the order of service and style of liturgy. Some scallywag, Scots no doubt, passed on the tip that pleading 'Church of Scotland' faith would get me off the parades, and it worked. For some strange reason, God forgave me for that and a thousand other blemishes on my record, as I did my own version of 'walking in the wilderness' for my nine years of military service.

My early exposure to Christian teachings stayed with me throughout my life despite glaring prolonged absences from the church family. My journey has seen migrations through numerous denominations over the years and I am more comfortable with today's much less dogmatic services. The almost 'rock and roll' tempo, high decibel output of music and relaxed modern style of praise in the Church I now attend would have caused shock and disdain in my grandfather's era of the Wee Free Kirk.

Despite sporadic, cyclical church affiliation, God was there for me when I needed Him most in a near-death air crash. I believe He guided my rescuers and care-givers and gave me the strength to overcome that tragic event. He restored my belief in Him. That day He affirmed, once and for all, in case I'd forgotten, that God is Good.

Demob and Beyond

*T*he difficult transition from military to civilian life has brought its challenges throughout history. I'm sure the Roman soldier who stood guard on Hadrian's Wall facing the dour Scots experienced radical change on his return to the Piazza in his native land.

Homeward bound British servicemen demobilized after World War II showed their ecstatic joy when discarding their khaki uniforms in favour of the postwar discharge-issued 'Grey Flannel Suit'. Scenes of the jettisoning of much-maligned military uniforms, from railway carriages leaving London for the north, were commonplace at that time.

Demob, after nine years in the Royal Army Medical Corps, also brought immense change in my life. I'd been granted a final three-month refresher course back at the physiotherapy school at

Woolwich after I left Iserlohn. During that time at the old Herbert Hospital I quickly realized that my fun and adventures in far off places had lowered the knowledge level I'd achieved when I qualified five years earlier.

Furthermore, it was a shock to realize that my professional experience in those years had been limited to treating a narrow range of patients with mainly musculo-skeletal injuries. This awareness was brought home painfully when I was asked to give a half-hour talk to fellow students during my second day back in school. My topic was, 'Treatment of a six year old child with Cerebral Palsy'. I ran out of words after thirty seconds.

Most of us on that refresher course got down to serious, almost frantic, study to better prepare ourselves for what lay ahead in our chosen careers. I look back now and am immensely grateful for that special time in school. Despite the glaring evidence of inadequacies in our current knowledge, we blithely applied for posts in civilian hospitals, offering glowing, embellished, resumes that we hoped would not come back to haunt us later.

My recent two years of close connection with the Canadian Military medical community in Germany, and the distant, fond, memory of my visit to Ontario as a Boy Scout, made me choose Canada as a focus for my employment inquiries. Whether it was the much-inflated description of my physiotherapy skills and experience, or simply that they were desperate for a new therapist, I landed a job offer from Sarnia General Hospital, in Ontario, which I quickly accepted by return mail.

To further complicate the radical changes that I was about to face, marriage too was on the agenda. Planning the wedding, emigration details, and intense studies made those three months flash past. I married Pip in Brighton and we left for Canada immediately thereafter.

Disembarking at Montreal from the cargo-passenger ship brought another surprise when my French dialect didn't work with the Quebec version I was hearing. Luckily my new job was in Ontario, not Quebec!

There were a myriad of challenges to be faced in the days and months ahead. Army life had not taught me anything about paying rent, furnishing an apartment, stocking a refrigerator, grocery shopping, or married life.

The purchase of Vespa #3 as a mode of transportation exhausted the cash reserves completely. The seemingly astronomical salary offer (compared to my army weekly wage) vanished faster than it came in, and the painful educational experience of living pay-cheque to pay-cheque became the new way of life. I recall with horror an incident that exemplified the absolute dearth of funds, waiting for the next payday. Stopping at an ice-cream stall, with my new wife by my side, I asked for two small cones. As I awaited the second cone, I placed my last dime on the counter assuming that would cover the total cost. (The year was 1966!) To my chagrin, the young server loudly stated that those ice-cream cones cost ten cents each. Apologetically, I told the server I didn't have any more money and watched as she made a great show of dumping that second cone in the garbage. Traumatized, we slunk off, scarred for life by the embarrassment.

Despite the hiccups and set-backs in that sunny southern Ontario city, life-long friendships developed and work was busy and rewarding. Social life, sports, and recreation brought balance and enjoyment in the new world. Even though everything settled into a comfortable routine, the old army 'posting' habit transferred into civilian life and new locations beckoned to me every two years or so.

First it involved a move to North Bay, Ontario where work at the Civic Hospital was a memorable stop-over. New friends and a beautiful, but cold, countryside offered rewards and challenges. Almost on schedule, Red Deer, Alberta became home for its two year saga, but it was, I suspect, doomed to failure by the lure of the Rocky Mountains on the western horizon. A superb learning and working experience in a private practice clinic, and the friendly prairie folks, were not enough to satiate my on-going wanderlust.

Finally, on July 1st, 1972, the world traveler put down roots in Cranbrook, BC. This location provided all I had dreamed about in the years before: Majestic scenery; friendly, welcoming neighbours;

and a rewarding six years as physiotherapist in the beautiful modern hospital, a far cry from my training days at the Royal Herbert that Queen Victoria had opened a century earlier.

My risk taking move to create, nurture, and develop a successful private practice in the Cranbrook Physiotherapy Clinic became the pinnacle of my professional career. Today, it gives me great pride, in my retirement, to see that practice still thriving thirty years later, under new ownership.

Along the way I was gifted with two wonderful sons, Ian and Craig. I also unfortunately underwent that all too common experience of divorce. Eventually I had the good fortune of a joyous second marriage to Maureen which has also brought me the delight of two step-children, Ryan and Jennifer. From this extended family, the continuing pride and delight has been the addition of ten grandchildren who help keep me young.

I have spent more than half my life in Cranbrook, and I believe that its people, and splendid four seasons, have made this an almost utopian homeland. Few can claim world-class hiking, windsurfing, kayaking, skiing, cycling and golfing within minutes of their door, in a friendly, welcoming, cultural community.

The wee boy from the Scottish glen has been blessed with much fun, frolic and good fortune in his three score years and ten.

Abbreviations
Used in the Book

I. Military Terms

AMRU	Army Medical Rehabilitation Unit
BAOR	British Army on the Rhine
KOSB	King's Own Scottish Borderers
KFS	Knife, Fork and Spoon
NAAFI	Navy, Army and Air Force Institute
NS	National Service
OG'S	Olive Green Uniform
QARANC	Queen Alexandra's Royal Army Nursing Corps
RAF	Royal Air Force
RAMC	Royal Army Medical Corps
REME	Royal Electrical and Mechanical Engineers

II. Military Ranks

NCO	Non-Commissioned Officer
L/Cpl.	Lance Corporal
Cpl	Corporal
Sgt.	Sergeant
S/Sgt.	Staff Sergeant
CSM	Company Sergeant Major

RSM	Regimental Sergeant Major
Lt.	Lieutenant
Capt.	Captain
Maj.	Major
Col.	Colonel
Gen.	General
TTO	Technical Training Officer

III. Other notations

An *   indicates the use of a pseudonym